design meets disability

design meets disability

Graham Pullin

The MIT Press   Cambridge, Massachusetts   London, England

MIT Press books may be purchased at special quantity discounts for business or sales promotional use. For information, please email <special_sales@mitpress.mit.edu> or write to Special Sales Department, The MIT Press, 55 Hayward Street, Cambridge, MA 02142.

This book was designed by the author and set in Joanna and DIN by the MIT Press. Printed and bound in the United States of America.

Library of Congress Cataloguing-in-Publication Data

Pullin, Graham, 1964–
Design meets disability / Graham Pullin.
    p. cm.
Includes bibliographical references and index.
ISBN 978-0-262-16255-5 (hard cover : alk. paper)
1. Design—Human factors. 2. Design. 3. Design, Industrial.
4. Engineering design. 5. Self-help devices for people with disabilities. I. Title.
NK1110.P85   2009
745.2—dc22
2008031030

10 9 8 7 6 5 4 3 2 1

Illustration credits are found on pages 323–328

To Mr. Cutler and Mr. Gross

contents

when the Eameses met leg splints   ix

thanks   xvii   introduction   1

initial tensions   11

fashion meets discretion   13

exploring meets solving   39

simple meets universal   65

identity meets ability   87

provocative meets sensitive   111

feeling meets testing   135

expression meets information   155

meetings with designers   181

Tomoko Azumi meets step stools   184

if Philippe Starck met bottom wipers   198

if Jasper Morrison met wheelchairs   200

Michael Marriott meets wheelchairs   202

if Hussein Chalayan met robot arms   216

Martin Bone meets prosthetic legs   218

if Jonathan Ive met hearing aids   232

if Paul Smith met hearing aids   234

if Cutler and Gross met hearing aids   236

Graphic Thought Facility meets braille   238

if Tord Boontje met braille   252

Crispin Jones meets watches for visually impaired people   254

if Durrell Bishop met communication aids   266

if Julius Popp met communication aids   268

Andrew Cook meets communication aids   270

if Dunne & Raby met memory aids   284

if Stefan Sagmeister met accessibility signage   286

Vexed meets wheelchair capes   288

conclusion   301

notes   309   photography credits   323   index   329

when the Eameses met leg splints

leg splint for the U.S. Navy designed in 1942 by Charles and Ray Eames, and manufactured by the Evans Products Company

good design on any terms

I eventually tracked down this iconic object in San Francisco, having long admired the contrast between its organic form and geometric holes, the combination of subtle surfaces and crisp edges. I am not describing a sculpture by Barbara Hepworth but rather a mass-produced product by Charles and Ray Eames. It is not even a piece of domestic furniture; it is a leg splint they designed for injured and disabled service personnel in the U.S. Navy.

The splint is made of plywood that has been formed into complex curves. Its design language was radical in 1942, and is still inspiring today. It appeals to me not because of its medical purpose but as good design on any terms. How many other examples of design for disability might that be said of? How often do we qualify, even excuse, design in this field because of the market for which it is intended? Perhaps this standard of design is not even considered appropriate?

DCW (dining chair wood) chair designed by Charles and Ray Eames in 1945, and manufactured by Herman Miller

disability inspires design

Charles Eames believed that "design depends largely on constraints."[1] It was the particular constraints of the U.S. Navy
brief that led the Eameses to develop their own technology
for forming plywood in complex curvature in the first place,
in order to make a lightweight yet stiff structure that accommodated the form and variation of the human body. But this
technique had a far-reaching influence on the future work of
the design partnership and design in general.

Organic plywood forms underpinned the iconic mainstream furniture manufactured by Herman Miller in the
1940s and 1950s, and through which the Eameses became
famous and influential. This sequence of events challenges the
so-called trickle-down effect whereby advances in mainstream
design are expected to eventually find their way into specialist products for people with disabilities, smaller markets that
could not have supported the cost of their development. Flow
in the opposite direction is just as interesting: when the issues
around disability catalyze new design thinking and influence a
broader design culture in return.

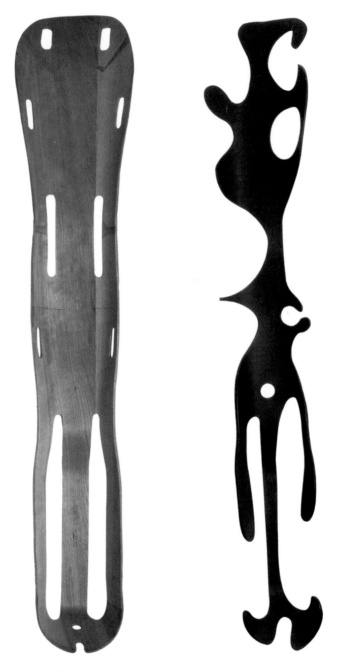

an original leg splint alongside a sculpture by Ray Eames

nurturing healthy tensions

The journey from leg splints to mainstream furniture was not a direct path. Ray Eames began by making (actual) sculptures out of spare leg splints, cutting into them with a jigsaw. She was exploring the visual languages that this new material could support, which was a natural mode of inquiry for an art school graduate—apparently playful, but with serious intent. Within the Eameses' work, two cultures existed side by side, in a healthy tension: the first directly solving problems and respecting constraints, and the second more open-mindedly, even playfully challenging these constraints and exploring further freedoms beyond them. The plywood furniture arose from both sides, from the splints and the sculptures.

Within design for disability, where teams still tend to come exclusively from clinical and engineering backgrounds, the dominant culture is one of solving problems. A richer balance between problem solving and more playful exploration could open up valuable new directions. The following chapters examine this and other tensions, each of which is currently biased in one direction, and each of which could benefit from a healthier balance.

thanks

It is only in writing these acknowledgments of course, that I realize quite how many people have been involved—and the considerable risk of leaving out someone really important by mistake.

First of all, thank you to the designers who took part in the discourses, giving their time and thoughts so generously: Tomoko Azumi, Michael Marriott, Martin Bone, Huw Morgan, Andy Stevens, Crispin Jones, Andrew Cook, Adam Thorpe, and Joe Hunter.

For other conversations, thank you to Aimee Mullins, Alan Newell, Amar Latif, Annalu Waller, Antony Rabin, Bill Gaver, Bodo Sperlein, Brian Grover, David Constantine, Duane Bray, Duncan Kerr, Durrell Bishop, Erik Blankinship, Fiona Raby, Graham Cutler, Hugh Herr, James Leckey, Jamie Buchanan, Jane Fulton-Suri, Johanna Van Daalen, Jonathan Ive, Julius Popp, Kelly Dobson, Michael Shamash, Norman Alm, Peter Bosher, Richard Ellenson, Roger Orpwood, Steve Tyler, Toby Churchill, and Tony Gross, and to many more for briefer or earlier conversations.

It is difficult to know how far back to go, but I would like to be able to thank my late father, whose joystick keyboards for disabled children first intrigued and inspired me. David Colven at the ACE Centre set my first brief at university, on a keyboard emulator for disabled kids; Roger Orpwood, Andrew Gammie, Mike Hillman, Jill Jepsom, Martin Rowse, Martin Breakwell, and Mike Broadhurst were among my colleagues at BIME, designing robot arms for people with spinal injuries; Duncan Kerr, Tony Dunne, Prue Bramwell-Davis, and Roger Coleman inspired me at the Royal College of Art, where I explored prosthetic hands; James Leckey, Alan Marks, and David Edgerley shared the design of the Woosh standing frame; Henrietta Thompson, Neil Thomas, Caroline Flagiello, Lucy Andrews, Anton Schubert, Paul South, and Neil Martin collaborated on HearWear; John Clarkson, Roger Coleman, Alastair MacDonald, and Elaine Ostroff have been supportive through the Include conferences; Alan Newell, Norman Alm, Iain Murray, Annalu Waller, and Rolf Black are fellow researchers into AAC at the University of Dundee; Andrew Cook is my research partner on Six Speaking Chairs.

For help in obtaining images and permissions, and within budget, I am grateful to the time and generosity of a number of people beyond the photographic credits, including Fiona Raby, Andy Law, Ben Rubin, Brandee Allen, Eugene Lee, Freddie Robins, Jasper Morrison, Johanna Van Daalen, Lucy Andrews, Shelley Fox, Stefan Sagmeister, Tord Boontje, and Violeta Vojvodic, for providing images; Aimee Mullins, Alice Panzer, Alison Lapper, Alison Walker, Bill Gaver, Catherine Long, Mat Fraser, David Maloney, Deirdre Buckley, Jacques Monestier, Li Edelkoort, Linda Nicol, Nick Knight, Platon, Sandy Marshall, Somiya Shabban, Susan Koole, Tricia Howey, and Trimpin, for kindly giving their permission; Anna Bond, Anna Smith, Beate Hilpert, Beth Gee, Carmen Marrero, Charlotte Wheeler, Chiho Sasaki, Chris McGinley, Cyril Wiet, David Hertsgaard, Esther Ketskemety, Genevieve Fong, Ingelise Nielsen, Jasmine Adbellatif, Jean-Claude Révy, Jill Wolfe, John Kirby, Kezia Storr, Kozue Ohyama, Laura Hitchcock, Laure-Anne Maisse, Liliana Rodrigues, Lourdes Belart, Luke Smith, Mabel Peralta, Mari Ikonen, Monica Chong, Nick Rapaz, Oliver Morton, Owen Davies, Pari Dukovic, Russell Simms, Sadie Watts, Sarah MacDonald, and Stéphanie van Delft for their help sourcing images. A special thanks to those who took photographs especially for this book: Mikkel Koser, Lubna Chowdhary, Barbara Etter, Paul Smith Ltd, Monica Chong, and Ssam Sung-un Kim.

For so much support at the start of the project, heartfelt thanks to Lorraine Shill and Matt Tabram. Thanks to Liz Brown and Henrietta Thompson for their early encouragement. At IDEO, among so many friends, thanks to Mikkel Koser, Colin Burns, Ingelise Nielsen, Bill Moggridge, Tim Brown, and to

Whitney Mortimer for connecting me with Caroline Herter. Thanks to Caroline Herter for connecting me with the MIT Press. At the University of Dundee, among so many colleagues and students on Interactive Media Design and Innovative Product Design and in the School of Design and the School of Computing, a special thanks to Alan Newell, Peter Gregor, and Terry Irwin.

At the MIT Press, thanks to Doug Sery for taking me on; Alyssa Larose for always being in touch; Yasuyo Iguchi for letting me loose on the design (what were you thinking?); Deborah Cantor-Adams and Cindy Milstein for making detailed editing so painless; and Gita Manaktala, Colleen Lanick, Susan Clark, Mary Reilly, Terry Lamoureux, Valerie Geary, Ann Sexsmith, and Ann Twiselton for their marketing talents and technical skills.

For trusted feedback and other help along the way, thanks to Alexander Grünsteidl, Amar Latif, Bernard Kerr, Bill Gaver, Colin Burns, Crispin Jones, Dan Schwarz, Hugh Aldersey-Williams, Henrietta Thompson, Jennifer Harris, Jon Rogers, Jonathan Falla, Luke Crossley, Martin Bontoft, Mike Press, Peter Bosher, Peter Gregor, Richard Whitehall, Roger Coleman, Rosalind Picard, Scott Underwood, Stephen Partridge, Steve Tyler, Tom Igoe, Tom Standage, Tomoko Azumi, Tracy Currer, and Vicki Hanson.

Lastly, the warmest thanks to Neil Martin, Andrew Cook, and Polly Duplock, for all your time, help, and support.

design meets disability

introduction

This is a book about how the worlds of design and disability could inspire each other. Over two decades, I have been part of these two worlds and their two distinct cultures. At a university and as a medical engineer I helped develop assistive technology for people with disabilities, in teams that were, and still usually are, made up of engineers, occupational therapists, clinicians, nurses, and other carers. After art college, as a design consultant, I led multidisciplinary teams of designers in creating products for consumer markets. I am struck by how distant those two worlds still are, yet how much more each could be influenced by the other.

on "disability" and "design"

First, let me offer a brief but necessary note about nomenclature. Any language used to describe the issues around disability is understandably—and rightly—politically charged. I have done my best to consult with disabled people and other experts, and have tried to adopt the most widely acceptable conventions. But conventions vary from country to country, between cultures and evolve over time—indeed, there have been several substantive changes in terminology over recent decades—so I hope they are (still) acceptable.

The World Health Organization recognizes *disability* "as a complex interaction between features of a person's body and features of the environment and society in which he or she lives."[1] Adopting the World Health Organization's classification, which will be discussed further in the chapter **identity meets ability**, I will use *impairment* to refer to "a problem in a body function or structure," whether motor, sensory, or cognitive. Even here the preferred language may vary from group to group; in Britain, the Royal National Institute of Blind People (RNIB) uses the term *visually impaired* people to encompass *blind* and *partially sighted* people, whereas the Royal

National Institute for Deaf People (RNID) uses the terms *deaf* and *hard of hearing* people as opposed to *hearing impaired* people.[2] The UK Government uses the term *learning difficulties* "to refer to individuals who have a general *cognitive difficulty* that affects their ability to learn," whereas in the United States, the Learning Disabilities Association of America provides support for people with *learning disabilities*.[3]

In the context of an environment or society that takes little or no account of impairment, people's activities can be limited and their social participation restricted. People are therefore disabled by the society they live in, not directly by their impairment, which is an argument for using the term *disabled people*, rather than *people with disabilities*, although each has its advocates, with the latter being known as *people first language*. I will use both, but given such complexity and sensitivity, I respectfully ask the reader to be patient with any inaccurate or inadvertently insensitive language you may find.

I find *design for special needs* a patronizing way to describe design specifically for people with particular impairments, but I will occasionally use this existing term, alongside alternatives that are unsatisfactory in other ways: *assistive technology* inappropriately puts the emphasis on the technology; *medical engineering* or *rehabilitation engineering* is limiting for reasons that will become obvious; and *design for people with disabilities* is not ideal because this could imply that no other design is. Examples of all four definitions include prosthetic limbs, wheelchairs, and communication aids—not that the word *aids* is satisfactory either. For balance, I will use the equally clumsy expression *mainstream design* to describe products designed for consumer markets often with the assumption that these consist entirely of nondisabled people. *Inclusive design* as it is known in Europe and Japan, or *universal design* in the United States, seeks to make mainstream design accessible to everyone.

I will use *design for disability* as a looser term, encompassing design for special needs, inclusive design, and other activities that challenge the division between designing for people with or without disabilities. Perhaps it would be more accurate to describe it as design *against* disability, as others have coined the term *design against crime*.[4] But design for disability sounds more neutral and understated, and the purpose of this book is not to introduce new nomenclature (with one exception, in the chapter **identity meets ability**).

In this book, the term *designer* will mean someone working broadly from an art school culture, whether by education or outlook. Examples include industrial designers, interaction designers, product designers, furniture designers, fashion designers, and graphic designers. I am choosing to turn the contrast up a little, because there is a clear distinction between this and an engineering culture, although in practice we are all less easy to pigeonhole as practitioners or people. The activity of *designing*, on the other hand, can be multidisciplinary or interdisciplinary, involving designers and people from technical, human factors, or clinical backgrounds—mechanical engineers, electronic engineers and technicians, human-computer interaction specialists, computer scientists and software engineers, ergonomists, cognitive psychologists and design ethnographers, clinicians, occupational therapists, physiotherapists, and nursing staff—and of course the people for whom something is being designed. Here I will try to avoid the term *user* because it sounds too functional, too focused on a task, whereas products also affect us by being owned, carried, or worn.

Within these definitions, this book touches on inclusive design, which brings issues of disability into mainstream design, but spends more time looking in the opposite direction, examining what would be gained by bringing an art school design culture to products specifically for disabled people. It argues for more designers to be involved in design for disability. Not just product designers but also fashion, furniture, and interaction designers; not just the most established designers but also the enfants terribles. These individuals might bring controversial influences to design for disability, but be provoked and influenced in return.

initial tensions

At the moment, there are significant differences between the cultures found within design and medical engineering—differences in values, methods, and even in ultimate goals. These differences tend to keep them apart, as two separate fields. And if the two were brought together to collaborate, these differences would undoubtedly set up real tensions within teams. Each of the first seven chapters in this book considers a distinct tension between the two cultures. Ultimately these could be harnessed as healthy tensions, the inevitable friction serving as a source of energy to catalyze new directions within each—perhaps even to fuse the communities together.

The first chapter, **fashion meets discretion,** examines a traditional goal of medical design to compensate for disability as discretely as possible. But might flesh-colored prostheses and miniaturized hearing aids send out tacit signals that impairment is something to hide? In contrast, a shift in perspective from corrective prescription to fashionable eyewear has been influential in helping to all but remove the stigma associated with wearing glasses. This has come about not just by involving the skills of designers but also by adopting the culture of fashion. Maybe medical engineering could embrace this culture elsewhere.

The second chapter, **exploring meets solving,** compares the problem-solving approach at the heart of medical engineering with more open-ended design exploration. The contrasts are illustrated by different kinds of chairs: wheelchairs, and the chairs exhibited at the Milan furniture fair. For many within design for disability, the latter epitomizes the worst excesses of mainstream design, yet it is a mechanism by which design experiments and progresses. Rare examples of this type of exploration being applied to disability are shown. Perhaps there might one day be wheelchairs at Milan.

The third chapter, **simple meets universal,** reconsiders the goals of inclusive design. A common assumption is that accessibility requires a redundancy of different sensory media. A definition of *design for the whole population* can also imply a flexible functionality, because different people may want to do different things. But this tendency to try to be all things to all people can lead to complex, compromised, and confusing products. In contrast, as individuals we often value design that is simple and fit for the purpose. An example of Japanese design illustrates that simplicity, not always comprehensiveness, has a role to play in accessibility.

The fourth chapter, **identity meets ability,** challenges the distinctions between inclusive design and design for special needs. Resonances can sometimes exist between the needs of people with a particular impairment and those of so-called able-bodied people in particular circumstances. Blurring these boundaries could change business models, but then demands a standard of design that a consumer market expects. Conversely, within populations of people with particular impairments, there may exist a diversity of attitudes toward their disability itself and about other issues. These cultural divisions should sometimes be respected and designed within, not across.

The fifth chapter, **provocative meets sensitive,** introduces the method of *critical design* that is provoking new thinking about issues as diverse as energy policy and antisocial behavior. Disability merits this attention. Critical design is often deliberately ambiguous and uncomfortable, and may employ humor, which could be considered insensitive. But countercultural groups within disabled populations are using dark humor to undermine unacceptable attitudes, and some have even started exploiting critical design themselves.

The sixth chapter, **feeling meets testing,** contrasts the roles of prototyping in design and clinical practice. The development of medical devices is underpinned by an established methodology of clinical trials that demands testing in controlled conditions. Meanwhile, designers increasingly view their role as creating not just objects but experiences too. A range of techniques has evolved called *experience prototyping*, informal methods that embrace the complexities of context and are difficult to quantify. Experience prototyping could play a valuable role alongside more formal methods, since the acceptability of any design for disability depends on the experience of living with it.

The seventh chapter, **expression meets information**, finishes with a frontier of design for disability: the development of communication aids for people with speech and language impairments. In a field dominated by technical challenges and the goals of supposedly *natural*, *transparent*, or *unambiguous* interaction, a role for designers is not even widely acknowledged. Yet aesthetics in the broadest sense is as fundamental here as elsewhere, because all the qualities of a communication aid—its sounds, appearance, and interactions—contribute to the shared experience of its use. These qualities send out their own messages.

meetings with designers

Having considered design and disability broadly, the book ends with a series of more detailed meetings: discussion of the contributions that leading designers might make, and discourses with individual designers about particular briefs. For those in medical design, these meetings may offer a glimpse of how diverse design culture is in its approaches and values, and therefore how much more varied the roles and contributions of designers could be. For designers, the ways in which fellow designers engage with the issues around disability might inspire similar or contrary thoughts.

Design and *disability* are each full of diversity, each somehow richer at an individual level than the collective. Disabled people do not all share a single experience of their impairment, and these experiences are inseparable from the rest of their lives; likewise, designers do not follow a single approach to design, and each designer will even approach different briefs in different ways. New directions will emerge when individual designers work on specific projects and with disabled people. This is likely to produce quite different results each time, but a richness of complementary and even contradictory responses is what design and disability still needs and deserves.

Seven longer discourses are interspersed with shorter speculations, juxtaposing well-known designers with briefs from design for disability, and asking: What might happen **if Philippe Starck met bottom wipers, if Jasper Morrison met wheelchairs, if Hussein Chalayan met robot arms, if Jonathan Ive met hearing aids, if Paul Smith met hearing aids, if Cutler and Gross met hearing aids, if Tord Boontje met braille, if Durrell Bishop met communication aids, if Julius Popp met communication aids, if Dunne & Raby met memory aids, and if Stefan Sagmeister met accessibility signage?**

The first of the longer discourses is **Tomoko Azumi meets step stools.** People with restricted growth can often find light switches and other fixtures out of reach, and some find it useful to carry around a set of folding steps. Designing lightweight yet stable folding steps is an engineering challenge in itself, but isn't a disabled person's experience of owning such a product so much broader? Azumi is a designer whose furniture has combined discreet mechanisms with simple and humane forms. Her first thoughts offer a glimpse of future possibilities, were design to meet disability.

The second discourse is **Michael Marriott meets wheelchairs.** Manual wheelchairs have advanced enormously in recent decades, converging with bicycles to share not only materials and components but also a common design language. Perhaps it was inevitable and appropriate that wheelchairs have come to emulate mountain bikes? Or perhaps there are alternatives. As a furniture designer who is equally passionate about chairs and bicycles, Marriott discusses the less obvious, more thought-provoking inspiration that bicycles could provide.

The third discourse is **Martin Bone meets prosthetic legs.** The form and function of prosthetic legs are often considered separately, with increasingly sophisticated damped or active mechanisms to assist walking, and designed to be worn with a flesh-colored cosmetic cover. Some amputees might choose to wear the mechanisms exposed, but as uncompromising pieces of technology. Or could prostheses be both honest and beautifully designed? Bone, an industrial designer at the consultancy IDEO, embraces a design philosophy that works outward from the inherent qualities of material. He discusses the materials he might select for a prosthetic leg, and what new forms might arise.

The fourth discourse is **Graphic Thought Facility meets braille.** The presence of braille in a public space sets up some intriguing contradictions: it can provide information to a minority of blind people who read it, becoming an almost abstract visual and/or tactile decoration for everyone else. What might be gained from taking both experiences into account, and how might this change the nature of inclusive design? Graphic Thought Facility (GTF) has designed information graphics for museums and exhibitions, but has also experimented with different materials and textures on the scale of print. GTF's early thoughts start to combine our visual and tactile experiences with, and counterintuitively, our distant and close-up perspectives of, braille.

The fifth discourse is **Crispin Jones meets watches for visually impaired people.** There is a long tradition of watches that can be read by blind people. Historically these were as exquisite as any watch, being made by the same watchmakers. Are modern alternatives, some with speech synthesis, designed with the same sensibilities? Jones is a designer and artist best known for his critical design pieces, which have included provocative reflections on the role of a watch. He considers the details of a tactile watch and the qualities that might be reflected back to its wearer.

The sixth discourse is **Andrew Cook meets communication aids.** The underlying technology of most communication aids is text-to-speech, and this is often the fundamental user interface as well. This can exclude those qualities of spoken language that are difficult to express in written language, especially the range and nuances of the tone of voice. Cook is a young interaction designer and computer musician whose work is exploring new, playful, and expressive interactions with computer-generated sound. We discuss applying these sensibilities to speech.

The seventh and final discourse is **Vexed meets wheelchair capes.** People who use wheelchairs outdoors need protection from the rain that keeps them dry while sitting and can also be put on while seated. Capes are a practical solution, but they are shapeless and redolent of hiking. Vexed's clothing is an extraordinary weave of urban culture, fabric technology, and political agendas. The designers at Vexed become inspired by thinking of wheelchairs in a broader context of urban mobility, alongside scooters and bicycles, and how a garment could be designed across these groups.

The book finishes with a **conclusion,** returning to the theme of creative tensions and the importance of looking beyond traditional views of function. It ends with the hope that examples as much as principles will soon bring about more mutual influence between disability and design, because design inspires design.

initial tensions

fashion meets discretion

Graham Cutler, Tony Gross, Alain Mikli, Sam Hecht
Ross Lovegrove, Nic Roope, Aimee Mullins, Alexander McQueen
Hugh Herr, and Jacques Monestier
spectacles and eyewear, hearing aids and HearWear
pink plastic legs and carved wooden legs, split hooks and golden hands

a memorable Cutler and Gross advertisement from the early 1990s

discretion

The priority for design for disability has traditionally been to enable, while attracting as little attention as possible. Medical-looking devices are molded from pink plastic in an attempt to camouflage them against the skin. The approach has been less about projecting a positive image than about trying not to project an image at all.

But is there a danger that this might send out a signal that disability is after all something to be ashamed of? If discretion were to be challenged as a priority, what would take its place? Invisibility is relatively easy to define, and may even be achieved through technical and clinical innovation alone, but it is more difficult to define a positive image purely from these perspectives.

fashion

Fashion, on the other hand, might be seen as being largely concerned with creating and projecting an image: making the wearer look good to others and feel better about themselves.

Eyewear is one market in which fashion and disability overlap. On the rare occasions that the words *design* and *disability* are mentioned in the same breath, glasses are often referred to as the exemplar of a product that addresses a disability, yet with little or no social stigma attached. This positive image for disability has been achieved without invisibility.

tension

Fashion and discretion are not opposites, of course; fashion can be understated, and discretion does not require invisibility. Nonetheless, there is a tension between these qualities because they cannot both be the absolute priority. There are also deep cultural tensions between the two design communities. Perhaps fashion with its apparent preoccupation with an idealized human form is seen as having little to say about diversity and disability. The extremes and sensationalism of cutting-edge fashion can seem inappropriate in the context of disability, where discretion is seen as being so important. For some in the medical field, the very notion of being in fashion, of designs coming and going, is the antithesis of good design.

But learning from fashion might require embracing not only its design qualities but also more of its values. Fashion does not just arise from a particular set of skills but creates and requires a culture. The mechanism through which fashion design evolves, whether through haute couture or street fashion, creates extreme designs that can provoke negative as well as positive reactions in different audiences. It may not be possible to have one without the other, to have the results without the culture and the values.

This chapter will consider the way that spectacles have evolved from medical aids to fashion accessories, reflecting on how this might inform the design of other products. In the case of hearing aids, this chapter looks at a recent initiative to inspire design research; in the case of prostheses, it anticipates such engagement in the future.

glasses

Glasses or spectacles are frequently held up as an exemplar of design for disability. The very fact that mild visual impairment is not commonly considered to be a disability, is taken as a sign of the success of eyeglasses. But this has not always been the case: Joanne Lewis has charted their progress from medical product to fashion accessory.[1] In the 1930s in Britain, National Health Service spectacles were classified as *medical appliances*, and their wearers as *patients*. It was dictated that "medical products should not be styled."[2] At that time, glasses were considered to cause social humiliation, yet the health service maintained that its glasses should not be "styled" but only "adequate."[3] In the 1970s, the British Government acknowledged the importance of styling, but maintained a medical model for its own National Health Service spectacles in order to limit the demand. In the meantime, a few manufacturers were offering fashionable glasses to consumers who could afford them. As recently as 1991, the design press declared that "eyeglasses have become stylish."[4]

These days, fashionable glasses are available in the shopping mall or on Main Street. It has been reported that up to 20 percent of some brands of glasses are purchased with clear nonprescription lenses, so for these consumers at least wearing glasses has become an aspiration rather than a humiliation.[5] So what lessons does this hold for design and disability? There are several, especially in relationship to the widely held belief that discretion is the ultimate priority in any design for disability.

First, glasses do not owe their acceptability to being invisible. Striking fashion frames are somehow less stigmatizing than the National Health Service's supposedly invisible pink plastic glasses prescribed to schoolgirls in the 1960s and 1970s. Attempting camouflage is not the best approach, and there is something undermining about invisibility that fails: a lack of self-confidence that can communicate an implied shame. It is significant that glasses continue to coexist with contact lenses, which do offer complete invisibility.

But neither is the opposite true: glasses' acceptability does not come directly from the degree of their visibility either. Brightly colored frames exist, although they are still a minority taste. This might serve as a caution to medical engineering projects that have adopted bright color schemes for medical products "to make a fashion statement" as the automatic progression from making a product flesh-colored. Most spectacle design, and design in general, exists in the middle ground between these two extremes. This requires a far more skilled and subtle approach—one that is less easy to articulate than these extremes. Designers often use the term *materiality* to describe the inherent aesthetic qualities of different materials. Materiality is hugely important to design in general and

camouflage eyewear by Cutler and Gross

spectacle frames in particular, yet it is so frequently absent outside a design culture. Manufacturers such as Alain Mikli are perpetually exploring new combinations of laminations, translucency, color, and decorative texture.[6]

And the most elegant frames can be let down by a badly resolved hinge detail or the way a nose bridge meets the frame. Everything is on display and contributing to the whole. Everything must be visually resolved—an attention to detail that is demanding even for the best designers.

eyewear

Spectacles have become *eyewear*, and this term encapsulates a number of important perspectives—perspectives that are currently missing from much design for disability. You *wear* glasses rather than carry or just *use* them. Somehow, the term *user* becomes inappropriate. *Wearer* sets up a different relationship between the designer and the person being designed for.

Of course, glasses are designed not as products in isolation but in relation to the body, and the most personal part of the body at that. This makes glasses' acceptability all the more impressive and encouraging. They frame not only their own lenses but more important, our face, eyes, and glances. With this comes the risk of a design not suiting a particular individual, or that individual not liking the design, and so the need for variety and choice.

This acknowledges the shift in perspective from a *medical model* to a *social model* of prescription. In the past, spectacles were seen almost exclusively in terms of their vision correction. This broader perspective acknowledges the significance of the perceptions of those around you: "What others see is more important than what you see yourself," as design writer Per Mollerup said of glasses.[7]

Eyewear positions glasses more as items of clothing than as products. A different approach, different references, and different designers spring to mind when thinking about glasses

Surround Sound Eyewear designed by Industrial Facility for RNID
HearWear project

in this way. Alongside specialist spectacle manufacturers, many fashion labels design and market eyewear collections. *Collections, labels,* and *brands*: these words set up different expectations and engagement from consumers. And *consumers* is a long way from *patients* or even *users.*

Fashion and trends become relevant. Materials and color play off clothing, accessories, and cosmetics; shapes work off hairstyles, not just bone structure. Wearers look forward to purchasing a new pair of glasses for the opportunity to try something different and reinvent themselves a little, as they might look forward to a change of haircut, or buying a new outfit or wardrobe of clothes.

Design becomes freighted with cultural references. Do these frames look rather 1970s? Are these flirting with bad taste? Designs can date and come back into fashion. Fashion moves forward through its avant-garde, be that couture or street culture. So embracing fashion necessitates going too far at times.

Eyewear designers Graham Cutler and Tony Gross have spent thirty years on the front lines of the revolution that turned eyewear "from medical necessity into key fashion accessory."[8] It is interesting to note how recent this revolution was, given how much it is now taken for granted. But Cutler and Gross describe themselves as the enfants terribles of optometry, and their role even now is to constantly test the limits of taste and style. Many of their frames refer back to vintage designs, and even play with past negative perceptions of glasses as nerdy and unfashionable. Nevertheless, Cutler and Gross glasses are always individual and glamorous, without being ostentatious (having no visible label), and their customer base transcends age and occupation.

This in itself is contentious. Many groups involved in design for disability subscribe to a culture of problem solving, evident in their methodology and work, and may even see fashion as the antithesis of good design. The thought of changing a hearing aid or prosthesis just because it had gone out

The Beauty of Inner Space designed by Ross Lovegrove for RNID
HearWear project

of fashion or its wearer fancies a change may be anathema to them. Certainly, fashion designers are rarely part of teams even developing wearable medical products, which is incredible considering the specialist skills they could bring as well as their experience and sensibilities. But if we are serious about emulating the success of spectacle design in other areas, we need to involve fashion designers, inviting them to bring fashion culture with them.

hearing aids

Compare glasses with hearing aids, devices developed within a more traditional culture of design for disability where discretion is still very much seen as the priority. Discretion is achieved through concealment, through a constant technological miniaturization. The evolution of the hearing aid is a succession of invisible devices: objects hidden under the clothing, in the pocket, behind the ear, in the ear, or within the ear. As the hearing aid has grown ever smaller, it has occasionally broken cover only to migrate from one hiding place to another. What has remained the same is the priority of concealment.

Such miniaturization has involved amazing technological development, but it is not without a price. Brian Grover, a technology expert at RNID, says that hearing aids' performance is still compromised by their small size and that they could deliver better quality sound if they weren't so constrained. This is how fundamental the priority of discretion can be. Yet for many hearing-impaired people, their inability to hear clearly is far more socially isolating than the presence of their hearing aid.

Where total invisibility is impossible, the last resort has been to mold hearing aids in pink plastic, betraying a white, Western bias in itself. Somehow this is the epitome of the medical model, perhaps echoed in the very term hearing *aid*. While this can set up an interesting countercultural appeal,

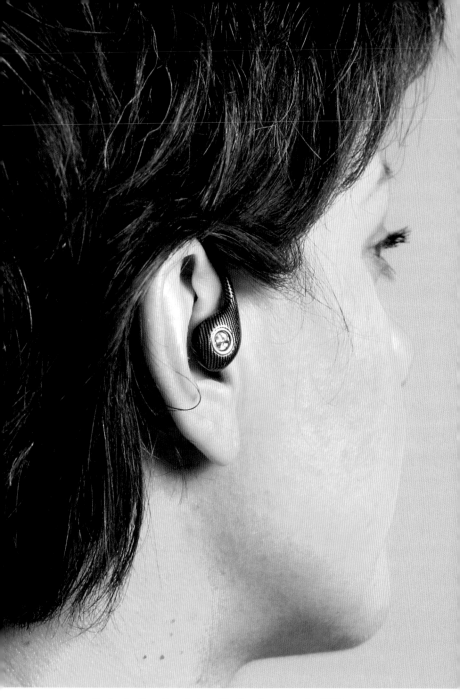

The Beauty of Inner Space designed by Ross Lovegrove for RNID

HearWear project

apart from the singer Morrissey, few people have been known to wear a hearing aid for show when they do not need one.

Recently, hearing technology manufacturers have discovered an alternative model. Many are turning to wireless cell phone earpieces as an example of positive imagery for technology worn in the ear from mainstream consumer product design. This is a welcome broadening of approach, but the mistake is to overlook the strong cultural associations of these devices—associations not easily perceived from within research and development departments: the trend for futuristic wireless earpieces in silver plastic with blue LEDs is aimed squarely at a technological early adopter, a market eager to emphasize its technical sophistication. These overtly technical products send out strong cultural signals that not everyone would be comfortable with, while largely ignoring the sensibilities involved in spectacle design.

HearWear

If anything, you might expect hearing aids to be less challenging than glasses: they don't obscure the face; there are strong traditions of ear adornment and jewelry in most cultures; and we all reach for earphones and headphones from time to time. But somehow, rather than adopting a diversity of design approaches, the hearing technology industry has remained conservative, perhaps because it is preoccupied with its perpetual technological development.

That is why RNID and Blueprint, the architecture and design magazine, launched HearWear, setting leading designers the brief to consider hearing aids and hearing technology from a fresh perspective. As Henrietta Thompson, deputy editor of Blueprint put it, "Over the decades there has been an amazing amount of technical development of hearing aids, but in that time little or no design investment has occurred."[9]

Hence the name HearWear, to emphasize a move away from considering hearing aids as technology. We had discussed

*WearHead*Phone* designed by Hulger for RNID HearWear project

whether *earwear* was more appropriate, being the direct analogy of eyewear, but opted for *hearwear* to open up the possibility of ideas that weren't just worn in the ear itself. One example is an experimental hearing aid developed in the United States that comprises an array of microphones on a necklace, providing high-quality, directional sound.

Sam Hecht of Industrial Facility is an industrial designer who has practiced in Tokyo, San Francisco, and London, and these influences combine in his typically strong yet quiet designs. Hecht makes the most direct connection with the design of eyewear by incorporating hearing technology into the arms of a pair of spectacles, with the arms branching to support integral earpieces. But he goes one step further than conventional hearing aid configurations, proposing an array of microphones, not just one on each side, thereby supporting superdirectional hearing when the signals from each are processed together. What it means to design a hearing aid changes if normal human ability is being surpassed, not just restored, and the design plays an additional role in expressing these augmented capabilities.

Product and furniture designer Ross Lovegrove brought his subtle, organic forms to a new visual language for wearable noise-canceling technology, in his response *The Beauty of Inner Space*. His design mixes biological forms appropriate for a prosthesis with the overt technology of carbon composite and the ambiguity of gold—at once a high-tech and traditional material with associations with both hi-fi and earrings. Like jewelry, the design seeks to complement the body rather than attempt to be camouflaged against it. Notice that the earphones are recessed to present an ear apparently open to sounds from the outside world, whereas a more convex form might have signaled that the wearer is listening to something else. The sparing use of gold at the earpieces accentuates their sensitivity.

Nic Roope of Hulger is known for the playful P*Phone, full-size retro telephone handsets that can be plugged into cell phones or computers for voice-over Internet protocol. The *WearHead*Phone* is an enormous set of headphones with a military camouflage paint job. Whatever the technical justification for their size, they also represent a supreme gesture of self-confidence—the antithesis of current hearing aids. The camouflage is a reference to street culture, but could also serve as an ironic commentary on the attempted camouflage of pink plastic hearing aids that are conspicuous but pretend to be invisible.

Of all the product designers who submitted concepts, seventeen in all, Hulger engaged with the brief in a way we would have seen more of had fashion designers also been invited. Fashion designers would probably have gone further still. Even after HearWear, there is still value in provoking yet more extreme approaches, just as eyewear is constantly pushing its own boundaries.

What the project demonstrated so successfully was that wherever an orthodox approach seems self-evident, there are always radical new perspectives that can challenge this. Designers are particularly skilled at breaking new ground in this way, but also at cross-fertilizing different fields. So ironically, medical engineering might particularly benefit from the involvement of designers who are not experts in medical products but bring fresh approaches from other consumer markets. And in turn, these designers would be afforded fresh perspectives to enrich and inspire subsequent work in their own areas.

bodywear

In many ways a more challenging area of design for disability is prosthetic limbs. Glasses are worn over the eyes, but they are not replacements for the eyes themselves. Similarly, hearing aids augment the ears. But prosthetic limbs are extensions of the body, not distinct products to be picked up and put down, and as such their design is more sensitive. In some ways it is the body itself that is being redesigned.

Given a challenge of this sensitivity, it is surprising to find that a role for any designer other than design engineers is not even widely acknowledged within prosthetics. A recent contract issued by the U.S. Defense Advanced Research Projects Agency to develop a prosthetic arm made no mention of anything needing to be *designed*, other than a human form and capabilities being achieved. Correspondingly, the call for proposals demanded an impressive multidisciplinary team of engineers, technologists, and clinicians, but made no mention of industrial designers or interaction designers, let alone sculptors.

legwear

A striking and memorable image of a different attitude to prosthetics is that of the athlete, model, and actress Aimee Mullins, seen here wearing her carbon fiber running legs, tracksuit bottoms, and nothing else. It is taken from the cover of the fashion magazine *Dazed & Confused*, an edition guest edited by fashion designer Alexander McQueen around a theme of fashion and disability, titled "Fashion-able?"[10] I have always liked this photograph for walking what I saw as a fine line between self-confidence and sensationalism. But in conversation, Mullins explains that it was not premeditated, and arose naturally out of a collaboration between McQueen, herself, and the photographer Nick Knight. "Our intention was to explore a body with a serious intent and create a beautiful image."[11] The pose and the clothing were aesthetic considerations.

Mullins could be said to have become an icon of the capable and glamorous disabled person, yet she is clear herself that the best thing she can do for people with disabilities is not to be thought of as a person with a disability. Returning to visual impairment, she admires Ray Charles as a musician,

Aimee Mullins photographed by Nick Knight for the cover of
Dazed & Confused, guest edited by Alexander McQueen

not for having been a blind man. Likewise, Mullins does not like being looked at as a *disabled* athlete, and has resisted what she refers to as a NutraSweet emphasis on achievement in the face of adversity.

The unashamed artificiality of Mullins's prostheses is still controversial (perhaps even more so when worn by a woman? But gender-related issues, among other significant political and economic concerns, are not the focus of this book). Their abstract elegance challenges the duality that has existed for so long between aesthetics and functionality. Conventional wisdom is that prostheses should either be made for *appearance*, so-called *cosmetic* limbs that are an accurate copy of the human body, with optimized functionality within this constraint, or for optimized *functionality* above all other considerations, as are tools. But Mullins's legs show this to be too simplistic. Her legs have a beauty of their own, not just as objects, but also in relation to her body and posture. Many attributes of even a functional prosthesis affect the image its wearer will project—implications that may not even be treated as conscious design decisions. But they could be, and designers could play a valuable role.

She thinks that fashion designers and jewelry designers should be involved in design for disability as a matter of course. "Discreet?" she sniggers. "I want off-the-chart glamorous!"[12] For her, modern luxury is less about a desire for perfection as a desire for options. Her wardrobe is made up not only of different clothes that can make her feel a different way but also different legs: there are her carbon fiber running legs, various silicone cosmetic prostheses, and a pair of intricately hand-carved wooden legs. "I'm thinking about what I'm going to wear them with: jeans and motorcycle boots, or my Azzedine Alaïa dress if I want to feel amazing."[13] Her legs too can make her feel amazing in different ways: a pair of silicone legs that are several inches longer than her own legs would be, make her (even) taller and more elegant on the catwalk,

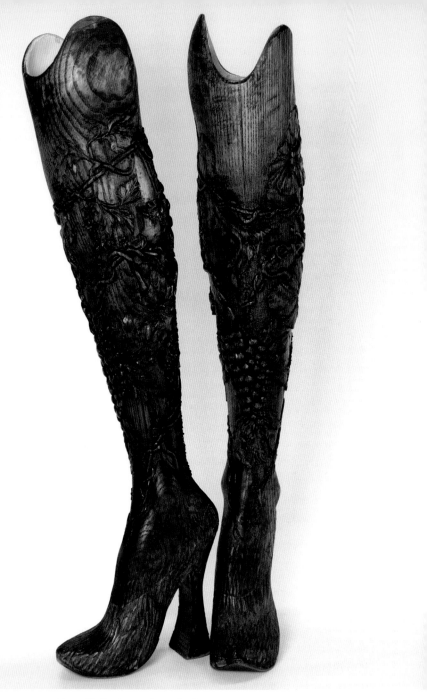

Aimee Mullins's carved wooden legs

while her eerie glass legs have an element of magical realism. This very choice becomes part of her individual identity and also a collective experience, shared with her friends: "Which ones are you wearing today, Aimee?" From the perspective of the health insurance companies, Mullins says that "every single pair of my legs are considered unnecessary." But an element of fantasy among the practicalities of everyday life is important to her. Even, as she wryly puts it, to express *a certain shallowness*.[14]

Someone with quite different attitudes to his prostheses, Hugh Herr, shared a platform with Mullins at the h2.0 symposium, subtitled "new minds, new bodies, new identities," that sought to blur the distinction between "able-bodied" and "disabled."[15] Herr heads the biomechanics group at the MIT Media Lab, where this event took place in May 2007. He lost both of his legs in a climbing accident when he was seventeen years old. As he came to terms with his disability, his prostheses became an important part of his self-image. But he still thought of himself as a climber, not an amputee. He fashioned himself climbing prostheses that gave him a foothold where others couldn't even gain a fingerhold, and telescopic legs that could be extended during a climb to be any length, shorter or longer than his original legs—even each leg a different length. Then he witnessed the reaction of his fellow climbers turn from pity to calls for him to be disqualified from competitive free-climbing for having an unfair advantage.

In those early days he was quite prepared to draw attention to his new legs, decorating them with polka dots in order to shock people. These days he's more restrained in both his dress and the aesthetics of his prostheses, but just as passionate about his team's work. If one individual's own attitudes have evolved over time, how much more does prosthetics need to embrace and accommodate a diversity of attitudes? Populations of people with disabilities can be every bit as diverse as society in general.

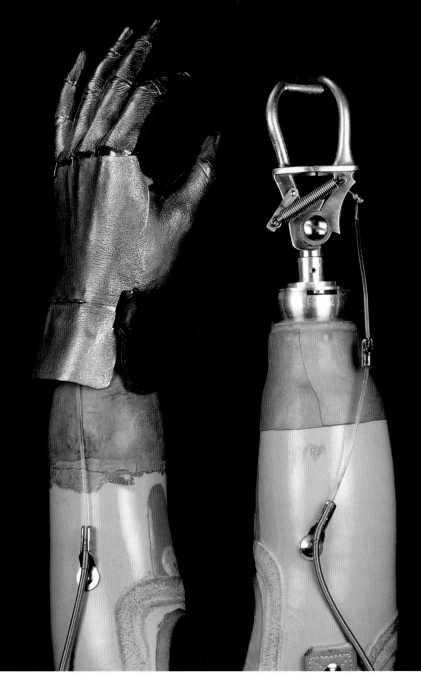

golden prosthetic hand by Jacques Monestier alongside a conventional
split hook

Herr agrees that art school–trained designers could play a valuable role as prosthetics moves forward, especially into exciting new territory in which human abilities are not just restored but surpassed. And when prostheses become not just replacement human limbs, then their design will help determine and communicate just what they are instead.

armwear

Prosthetic hands are even more intimate than prosthetic legs, yet again it seems that there are only two common approaches: those of *realism* and *functionalism*. The realistic approach is defined as a visual imitation of a human arm, and so the materials are chosen for their ability to be formed to visually represent human skin: PVC plastic and silicone in shades of pink and brown with molded wrinkles, nails, and sometimes even veins. But the static visual appearance is only one aspect of the aesthetics of any object. Some amputees have spoken of not liking the *feel* of their hand. They, like anyone, unconsciously cradle one hand in the other, yet the materials chosen for their visual resemblance to skin are rubbery and clammy to the touch, and can feel dirty somehow. Some amputees even complain that their prosthesis *smells* unpleasant.

The opposite, functional approach prioritizes how well a prosthesis works over how it looks, and has resulted in split hooks. These may work well as tools, but any hand is more than a tool—it becomes part of the wearer's body image, a visual as well as a functional termination of their arm. Yet the design of split hooks barely acknowledges the wearer's body or their clothing.

Sculptor and creator of automata Jacques Monestier has created a prosthetic hand that represents a provocative alternative to both hands and hooks; it is a design that simultaneously acknowledges its role yet also its artificiality. The back of his golden hand is cast in the likeness of a human hand, but from an alloy; the palm is upholstered in soft, luxuriant

golden prosthetic hand by Jacques Monestier

leather. As Monestier explains, "Amputees often suffer a loss of self-image. I wanted to transmute what might be considered a disfigurement into something marvelous and exotic. I wanted to create a hand that would no longer cause shame and repulsion. I wanted the amputees themselves to be proud to have a prosthetic hand and pleased to look at it. And for the people around them, I wanted the prosthetic hand to be an object of healthy curiosity, a work of art."[16]

Monestier worked with leading prosthetist Jean-Eric Lescoeur, but was also inspired by a sixteenth-century painting of a surgeon fixing an artificial hand to an injured soldier: "It was an armored gauntlet, like a golden hand. A beautiful, vibrant, quasi-mythical object—nothing like those dead, pink, plastic hands which pretend to imitate human flesh. This was the hand I wanted to create, with the added refinements of modern materials and technology."[17]

New possibilities need not be seen as a rejection of existing devices, which so many users are happy with: some prefer their prosthesis to be an overt tool; others feel most comfortable wearing no prosthesis at all; and others still do want the discretion of a cosmetic hand above all things. But some amputees are not so comfortable at present. I have talked with an amputee who didn't like wearing her prosthesis because it would initially "fool" new acquaintances, for them only to realize later it was artificial, and she dreaded reading their moment of realization. Monestier's hand gets this moment out of the way right at the start.

It seems important to continually challenge existing approaches, just as this is the way in which every other area of design, art, and science progresses. All too often attitudes are spoken of as if homogeneous. "Amputees want discretion." Well, not everyone. Not always.

embracing fashion

The evolution of glasses from medical appliance to fashion accessory challenges the notion that discretion is always the best policy. Hearing aids, prostheses, and many other products could be inspired by this example. More confident and accomplished design could support more positive images of disability.

Eyewear has come about by adopting not just the language of fashion but also its culture. If medical design wishes to emulate this success in other areas, it needs to appreciate that fashion often moves forward through extreme and even controversial work, and to welcome this influence within design for disability. We have to do more to attract fashion designers to collaborate on designs for people with a disability, and bring their perspectives to both the practice and culture of inclusive design. At times this will expose cultural differences, but these are healthy tensions, well worth embracing and harnessing.

exploring meets solving

Marcel Breuer, Shin Azumi, Tomoko Azumi, Jasper Morrison
David Constantine, Shelley Fox, Li Edelkoort, and Bodo Sperlein
Bath chairs and Gouty chairs, chairs and wheelchairs inspired by bicycles
chairs from Milan, chairs from Japan and wheelchairs from Cambodia
Blind design and braille for the sighted

chairs designed by a diversity of international designers for the
nextmaruni collection

solving

Disability can lead to problems in people's lives, either directly or indirectly. These problems are either viewed as being inherent in an impairment itself, or as being created by the designed environment and other people's behaviors. The respective terms people with disabilities and disabled people (people disabled by the society they live within) emphasize each of these perspectives. Either way, exclusion and discrimination remain serious problems at both an individual and a social scale.

The educational background of medical engineers attunes them to problems. A typical engineering methodology might start with *Step 1: problem definition*, followed by *Step 2: solution generation*, and so on. Some theorists even try to define *design* in its broadest sense as *problem solving*. Because of the nature of disability and the culture of engineering, design for disability and inclusive design are usually approached as an exercise in problem solving, as can be seen from respected books on the subject. This also has something in common with the clinical tradition of diagnosis and treatment.

But what if some of the challenges facing design for disability were not best described as *problems* to be *solved*? And are issues not easily defined as problems likely to be overlooked? Might valuable new directions emerge only by adopting quite different approaches?

exploring

Not all design is about solving problems. Designers may revisit an object, a material, or a medium that has already been successfully designed, designed with, or designed within many times before, in which case the value does not lie in solving an unsolved problem. Many art school disciplines involve exploration that can appear playful and open-ended, but its intent may be no less serious for this.

Gouty chair from around 1800, for people with gout

Design exploration may still require solving problems that arise along the way, but frequently as a means to an end rather than as an end in itself. This is a subtle yet fundamental inversion of engineering methodologies that will usually include a creative exploration of alternatives, though as a means to the end of solving the core problem.

Beyond an individual project or the work of an individual designer, designers responding to or reacting against each other's experiments advances design as a discipline and a culture. Designers learn as much by being inspired as from being informed.

tension

Designers' obsession with endlessly exploring details—details that the public may not even consciously notice—can lead to accusations of self-indulgence, of designing for themselves and not for others. In the field of disability, where so many real yet soluble problems are still unsolved, how could more open-ended exploration ever be justified within the limited resources available?

Again, our language can skew the debate. Describing design as problem solving implies a tactical activity, albeit an important one, whereas broader definitions can recognize an investment more akin to technical or clinical research. Later chapters will consider design's role in provoking discussion and changing attitudes.

Many within design for disability view their field as the antithesis of what they see as the irresponsibility of mainstream design and somehow in opposition to this. I have heard a leading figure in accessibility research and development announce that he had chosen not to involve any designers in his team because he wanted "solutions that were *usable*, not just *pretty*." This misguided statement implies that design has no role beyond beauty and that beauty has no role in design for disability.

Bath chair from around 1900

In return, many designers see design for disability as part of engineering and human factors, and perceive disability in terms of approaching legislation that threatens to compromise their creativity, rather than as a source of fresh perspectives that could catalyze new directions and enrich the whole of their work.

There is not so much a clash of design cultures as a yawning gulf between them. The result of this distance is that industrial and interaction designers, fashion designers, and furniture designers are unlikely to be part of the teams designing products, interfaces, clothing, or furniture for people with disabilities. Sometimes this is an oversight, but at other times it stems from a deep cynicism about art school design disciplines. And this situation is being perpetuated: it is still more likely that an engineering undergraduate will attempt to design a wheelchair than will a furniture design student; it is more likely that a computer science student will attempt a communication aid than that an interaction design student will do so. Design for disability would benefit from a better balance of these complementary approaches, whereas at the moment one dominates almost to the exclusion of the other.

This chapter will start by illustrating these contrasting cultures through related products that epitomize each: wheelchairs and chairs. The wheelchair has become the icon of disability, to the extent that accessibility signage uses a person in a wheelchair to represent disability in general. The chair in its many forms is a design standard, perpetually reinterpreted by successive designers. Later I will consider particular examples of open-ended exploration and their value to design for disability.

wheelchairs converge

The history of wheelchair design is revealing.[1] In the eighteenth century in the French royal court, wheelchairs or *roulettes* were considered stylish enough to be used by disabled

Wassily chair, designed by Marcel Breuer in 1925 and manufactured
by Knoll

and able-bodied alike.[2] In nineteenth-century England, Bath chairs were a fashionable form of transportation for wealthy visitors to spas and seaside resorts.[3] These wood and wicker chairs owed much to contemporary conservatory furniture, exhibiting similar styles and an equivalent degree of stylistic variation—a closeness to mainstream furniture design that is absent today.

In 1932, the company Everest & Jennings developed a tubular steel wheelchair, a breakthrough in strength and portability. At the time it also evoked modernism, sharing this new material with the Wassily chair designed by the Bauhaus tutor Marcel Breuer in 1925 and the cantilevered MR chair designed by the architect Mies van der Rohe in 1927. But later, in the 1950s, while domestic furniture moved on to the molded plywood and fiberglass forms of the Eameses and Robin Day, the wheelchair remained the same. Its utilitarian chromed construction became more reminiscent of hospitals, where tubular metal remained prevalent for hospital beds and trolleys, IV stands and crutches, and thereby reinforced the *medical model* of disability as a condition to be *cured*, not the *social model* that acknowledges wider social and cultural issues.[4]

In the 1970s, following the war in Vietnam, the Veterans Association in the United States successfully lobbied for investment in wheelchairs better suited to young, otherwise active war veterans, challenging a previous stereotype of wheelchair users as elderly women. There followed an impressive application of space technology and, perhaps appropriately, military-specification materials. The result was lighter, more carefully balanced wheelchairs, often less inherently stable but more maneuverable by an occupant with good upper-body strength. Another manifestation was an explosion in wheelchair sports, including basketball and marathon racing, frequently using specialist chairs with further functional refinement.

For any wheelchair these days, the functional requirements are onerous. Its weight and center of gravity are crucial

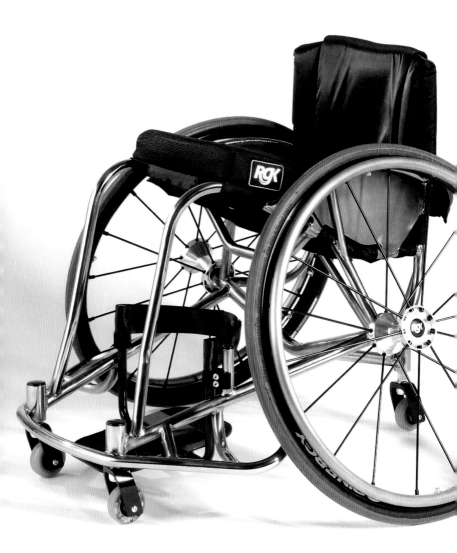

RGK Interceptor wheelchair

to maneuverability and stability, yet it may also need to be transported empty, perhaps folding up in some way. Postural support is more critical than for a normal chair because occupants are seated for longer at a time, are more immobile, and their condition may make them prone to pressure sores. A diversity of clinical needs, requiring adjustment, modularity, or customization, can complicate things still further. This complex set of requirements can understandably dominate any further design issues. A brief as technical as this is more likely to be tackled by an engineering design team than a furniture designer, and more likely by an undergraduate at a technical university than by an art school student. Wheelchairs have become finely engineered machines not just because of their function but also because of the skills and aspirations of the designers that have been attracted to designing them.

Wheelchairs have converged in their resemblance to modern bicycles, especially the mountain bike. They already share components such as spoked wheels, brakes and handlebar grips, and a construction from tubular alloy, but in the choice of finishes, colors, and graphics, further opportunities are taken to adopt the same design language. This lends the reassuring familiarity of a mainstream product, and sets up positive associations with mobility, fitness, and ability. Surely this is the ideal conclusion to the wheelchair's aesthetic evolution?

Well, perhaps this convergence is not altogether welcome. Johan Barber has noted that the current homogeneity of the appearance of wheelchairs can hide the individuality of the user.[5] Should individuality be part of the design brief, and what would we mean by this? Should it be individuality for the sake of differentiation, or something relating to the existing identity of the person sitting and living in that chair? Despite indisputable progress, there is an extent to which we have replaced one stereotype of a wheelchair user with another—a frail older woman for an athletic younger man.

Gentleman's chair built by William Dickson in 1989, and restored by
Ryan McLeod, Jamie Shek, and Ian Shiels

diverse chairs

In contrast to this convergence in wheelchair design, the evolution of the chair continues to generate increasing diversity.

The Milan furniture fair and the NeoCon world's trade fair in Chicago are among the events at which contemporary furniture is exhibited and celebrated. Each year, designers, manufacturers, retailers, journalists, and an interested public converge on Milan to see the launch of new designs for seating and lighting. While some new chairs each year depend on advances in materials and production techniques, progress is not measured in terms of technology. Many new arrivals will be variations or reflections on previous designs, involving new ideas or expressing new values.

This proliferation is reflected in books with titles like *1000 Chairs* and *1000 Lights*, but it provides much more than an overwhelming choice for the consumer.[6] One of the ways that design progresses is through *standards*. Designers return to ubiquitous products like chairs and lights in much the same way that musicians revisit and reinterpret old tunes. And this is not restricted to furniture design and industrial design; my interaction design students have recently used chairs as a medium to explore new interactive exhibits in a project called *Forgotten Chairs*.[7] Outside a design culture, this obsession can be misinterpreted: the familiar criticism, "Does the world need another chair?" is a little like asking, "Does the world need another version of 'A Night in Tunisia'?" As much as being a new product, each chair is a mechanism by which new approaches to design are explored and new design languages disseminated—approaches and languages that can then be applied to other products as well as to chairs. Many respected and famous designers have chairs to their name, whatever else may have been the focus of their careers, whether architecture or products rather than furniture. These chairs often embody a distillation of their design philosophy, and by serving as a

leather and wood chair designed by Shin Azumi and Tomoko Azumi
for the nextmaruni collection

common medium, illuminate comparisons between different designers that might not otherwise be so evident.

Japanese manufacturer Maruni launched no fewer than ten different chairs at once in its nextmaruni collection. Acknowledging the relatively recent presence of the chair in Japanese furniture, it commissioned ten leading designers to each define an *archetypal* Japanese chair. Each response combined elements specific to the brief—the designer's interpretation of the essence of a chair, wood as a material, and Japanese design—with elements of his own personal philosophy that he might have applied to other products. And in turn, a brief like this has the power to influence a designer's philosophy in the future.

For the London-based Japanese designers Shin Azumi and Tomoko Azumi, a Japanese aesthetic resides in the way in which "consideration and attentiveness are present to an astonishing degree while, on the surface, an expression of utter simplicity is maintained."[8] At first sight their chair looks beautiful yet austere, offering visual minimalism but not promising comfort. On further investigation, however, its simple flat panels prove not to be made from a hard laminate as they appear but instead are yielding, upholstered leather cushions.

For English furniture designer Jasper Morrison, the nextmaruni project revealed the thought given to an object's beauty in Japan. In the West, he says, discussion about design is usually limited to "It's beautiful" or "It's very ugly." Sometimes the conversation will progress to the level of "It's beautiful, I really like the shape and the way the materials are combined," but as Morrison explains, "we might look strangely at someone who analyses an object in more depth than this."[9]

Certainly, for some in design for disability, such preoccupations would represent all that is wrong with mainstream design: a degree of obsession that could be seen as self-indulgent, self-referential, and devoid of relevance to the profound issues that design faces—one of which is exclusion on the basis of

chair designed by Jasper Morrison for the first nextmaruni collection

a disability. What is the value in pursuing diversity, seemingly for its own sake?

diverse wheelchairs

Diversity already plays an important role in some areas of design for disability, though. Motivation is a charitable organization that designs and builds wheelchairs in low-income countries.[10] In each country it visits, twenty in the last twelve years, Motivation has established sustainable local manufacture, which means that any wheelchair must be appropriate to that country and community. This has resulted in a different chair design in each country, based not only on local needs, and the prevalent types of disability and terrain, but also on local manufacturing skills.[11]

These pragmatic goals have resulted in a rich diversity of wheelchair designs. In different countries, Motivation's chairs employ different layouts, geometries, constructions, and components—for example, the different wheel sizes are dependent on the prevalent local bicycle wheels, so that spares are readily available. Its wheelchair for Bangladesh owes a lot to Western wheelchair design, with a welded metal frame, albeit with an unusual diagonal design that simplifies its construction, whereas the chair developed for Cambodia has a distinctive hardwood frame because of the local materials. Furthermore, the rough terrain in Cambodia dictates a three-wheeled layout with a central wooden spine supporting a single front wheel.

The aesthetic of each wheelchair is quite different: some allude more to a conventional wheelchair or bicycle design, and others to local domestic furniture. And as the design changes, so the spatial and visual relationship between the chair and the user's body is changed. The user's posture within the chair, actual and apparent, changes between four- and three-wheeled layouts as well as between different-size wheels.

Motivation founder David Constantine, speaking in England, brings up the social significance of seating posture in

wheelchair designed by Motivation in tropical hardwood for local
manufacture in Cambodia

wheelchairs. He finds his own wheelchair perfect for the office, where it puts him on a level with his colleagues around a meeting table. But at home he can feel as though he is sitting to attention, with his friends relaxing below him in armchairs and on sofas. A wheelchair that let him slouch at that level would help him to feel more comfortable.

Could and should some of this diversity be brought back to wheelchair design in Europe and North America, as a tool to break away from conventional solutions and open up new directions, or even as a goal in itself, in order to increase variety and choice? Would it be inappropriate to apply inspiration from this low-income program to a more affluent Western market? Could the concerns of the Milan furniture fair ever be relevant when pressure sores are still so prevalent, even here? But moving from a medical to a social model of disability means acknowledging the importance of both clinical and cultural issues when designing wheelchairs. Not one at the expense of the other, but both.

chairwear

If spectacles have become eyewear and hearing aids earwear or HearWear, what shift in approach might the term *chairwear* inspire? Could it inspire thinking of someone as a wheelchair's *wearer*, not just its user, rider, or passenger? A wheelchair is a frame in which you and your clothing are seen. It is the place from which you receive guests. It is what you go out on the town in. Each of these associations conjures up issues and thoughts not provoked by thinking of wheelchairs exclusively as transportation. And each suggests different types of designers with whom to explore new directions.

How different the situation would be if the wheelchair became one of the design standards that designers sought to reinvent, alongside the dining chair and the armchair. This more than anything would connect the Milan furniture fair and NeoCon to exhibitions of so-called equipment for the

Braille Dress by Shelley Fox

disabled such as Naidex in the United Kingdom or RESNA in the United States. What if leading wheelchair and furniture manufacturers such as Quickie and Herman Miller collaborated with each other and commissioned leading furniture designers? How different if one could go to Habitat or Knoll to browse the latest trends in wheelchairs, not just a specialist retailer of aids for daily living. Perhaps the most interesting wheelchair designs would occasionally be offered as variants with legs, for jealous ambulatory consumers, because approaching chair design from the direction of wheelchair design would lead to new ideas.

Similarly, other design events have a natural affinity with other products for disabled people, such as Paris fashion week with hearing aids or Ars Electronica with communication devices for people with speech impairments. The potential range of manufacturers and designers could be diverse and challenging; it is interesting to speculate how fashion designers like Issey Miyake might change forever the way fabrics are employed within medical engineering. More ideas for design collaborations are discussed later in this book.

With even more profound implications for the future, we might look forward to the best young design students being drawn in—not just those destined for mainstream commercial success but also the enfants terribles. We would benefit from attempts to undermine our preconceptions of what a wheelchair should be, whereas at the moment, design for disability often attracts students seemingly more motivated by user-centered design than by stirring up design itself. The irony is that design for disability needs both types of young designer.

designing braille for the sighted

This argument relates as much to the environment we all share as to products for people with disabilities and as much to inclusive design as to design for special needs. To give one example, when braille is employed in inclusive design, rather

INTERIOR
VIEW 14

blind design

Interior View 14, "Blind Design"

than in publications or products specifically for people who read braille, it inevitably becomes part of the visual and tactile experience of sighted people—a visible, if illegible, part of their environment. We need designers to explore new *visual* languages that might emerge when braille is combined with visual information and even decoration. Seeing this as a *problem* to be *solved* is probably not the best frame of mind with which to engage with it. Here are the beginnings of more playful approaches.

The artist and designer Shelley Fox has repeatedly explored braille and Moon writing in her work. (Moon is another form of embossed writing, derived from simplified letterforms from the Roman alphabet, and so mainly used by people who lose their sight as adults, already having learned how to read.) She was inspired by and has become slightly obsessed with both, sending out Moon invitations to her private shows for guests to decipher and abstracting braille into knitted clothing. These woolen abstractions of braille are illegible to visually impaired people, yet provoke reflection on the inevitable role of braille as visual and tactile *decoration* in the eyes of a sighted audience. Fox's work may not be directly related to accessibility but could inspire future work that is. The best inclusive design depends on addressing this secondary agenda, just as the best of any design is enhanced by necessary elements, not compromised by them.

Even more indirectly, Li Edelkoort's magazine, *Interior View*, featured an edition called "Blind Design."[12] This was not, as its title might suggest, about design for visually impaired people but instead a more diverse collection of design inspired by visual neutrality, texture, or tactility. An exploratory concept for a telephone has raised bumps for keys, yet none of these are labeled and there is no screen. It is interesting to show the visual promise to a *sighted* audience of adopting a tactile design—a perspective that can turn design for disability into truly inclusive design. A sighted user, too, might

plates with texture by Bodo Sperlein

be intrigued and delighted by a design that does not rely on visual explanation.

Another page shows a bone china plate with a texture reminiscent of braille. The designer, Bodo Sperlein, was exploring how this texture can define the design, and what its relationship is to the overall mass and surface. But this is it not braille, and it was not even inspired by braille but rather by "the fluidity of the material."[13] And yet, this work has something to say about integrating braille in the design of accessible though beautiful objects and interiors—far more to say, indeed, than current lifts and elevators in which braille is so obviously applied as an afterthought and with no sense of its visual impact; as a regulatory requirement, not an opportunity for influencing the whole. The highest goal today seems to be that braille should not overly detract from the environment, rather than that it could ever enhance it. Whereas Sperlein "wanted to invite people to touch the plates, and also to intrigue them."[14]

Inclusive design demands these profound new perspectives; it deserves the involvement of our leading designers. When designing braille into the visual environment, it may be more appropriate to consider it as much from a decorative as a practical point of view. We *do* need solutions that are *pretty* (among all kinds of other qualities) not just usable.

In this instance as in many others, it may actually be most appropriate to involve designers who are not experts in inclusive design at all, nor who even wish to become specialists. My recommendation is for inclusive design to become more open to attracting and absorbing diverse positive influences, to adapting and adopting more radical approaches, even those that may not at the moment be producing inclusive results. Nor is this contradictory to inclusive design's role of exerting a strong influence on design. Quite the opposite: the more cross-fertilization there is, the more mutual influence there can be.

keeping the design in design for disability

If there is a welcome change in our approach to disability, from a medical to a social model, it follows that the role of design needs to change too, and therefore the nature of design teams must change as well. Design processes need to become more inclusive in several ways, involving not only disabled people themselves but also a greater diversity of designers.[15] If we aspire to the qualities and quality of mainstream design, this will require the sensibilities as well as the skills of those who create mainstream design. Art school design disciplines are as essential to the mix as engineering and human factors.

Mediocrity must be avoided. In design for special needs, mediocrity can result in people being further stigmatized by the very products that are intended to remove barriers for them, thereby undermining the highest goal of social inclusion. In inclusive design, any inclusive but otherwise mediocre design might only prove attractive to users who are currently excluded. If so, it would become design for special needs by default.

If design for disability positions itself as something quite distinct, even somehow in opposition to mainstream design, it will inevitably be less influential. An implicit message that designers have no part to play in design for disability will become a self-fulfilling prophesy. If design for disability seeks to marginalize design in general, it will marginalize itself instead. If many designers are not engaging with disability, seeing only an encroaching legal obligation that will stifle their creativity, the way to change these attitudes is by more collaboration, not less.

It is important that we keep the *design* in design for disability. This might prove as challenging within design for disability as disability can be within a wider design community, but it is a challenge that both cultures need to rise to.

simple meets universal

Jonathan Ive, Steve Tyler, Bruce Sterling, Christopher Frayling
James Leckey, Steve Jobs, Roger Orpwood, and Naoto Fukasawa
Apple iPod and *Apple iPhone, gizmos and spimes*
the flying submarine and the Woosh chair, simple radio and Muji CD player

Apple iPod shuffle

universal

Design for disability is often under pressure to be universal. On the one hand, when designing for special needs affecting small percentages of the population, there is a strong business argument not to further fragment the potential market. The next chapter, **identity meets ability,** will challenge whether it is appropriate for a single design to accommodate everyone with a particular disability.

Within inclusive design, on the other hand, the contention may be one of principle. Also known as *universal design*, inclusive design has been defined as *design for the whole population.*[1] This definition mixes two issues: the first is that different people have different abilities, and so may be excluded if a design is not accessible to them; and the second issue is that different people have different needs and desires *irrespective of their abilities*, and so may just want different things from any product or service.

The first issue is often addressed by multimodal interfaces with a redundancy of visual, audible, and tactile cues to accommodate people with impaired touch, hearing, and/or sight; the second is frequently handled by multifunctional platforms containing many features in an attempt to accommodate as broad a range of uses as possible. Surely the more a product does, for more people, the more inclusive it can be said to be. But does this type of universal design then risk becoming a complicated design? And how inclusive is it then?

simple

As individuals rather than populations, we may take a different perspective. In an increasingly complex world, we value simplicity in many forms: functional, visual, and interactive. *Fitness for purpose* not only implies that something does what it needs to well but also that it is not compromised by doing more than it has to; a design pared down to the minimum can be quiet, yet iconic; and the simplest of interactions can

Apple iPod

be refreshingly direct and immediate. We perceive and appreciate the thoughtfulness that lies behind an elegant design.

tension

Both qualities sound admirable, but once again there is a tension between them that needs to be confronted. Despite a proliferation of technology and consumption that is so worrying in other ways, many people remain excluded and disabled by design that does not acknowledge their abilities. And being seen to be user centered can also imply incorporating the needs and desires aired at early focus groups—a pressure reinforced by consumer markets that compete on the basis of so-called features.

So should comprehensive functionality take precedence over simplicity? Or should we disentangle the two aspects of universality, separating the effects of disability from the wish to design anything to be *all things to all people?* What might the effect on inclusion be if we placed more emphasis on simplicity?

This chapter starts with a familiar example of a simple yet popular design, and then hears several different voices discussing the balance. It ends with an extreme trade-off between simplicity and universality—one that could inspire alternative aspirations for inclusive design in the future.

icon of simplicity

Apple's iPod is as good a candidate as any for a product that epitomizes good design, as understood by both the design profession and the public. It has earned the most prestigious international design awards, the ultimate peer recognition for designers: iF, IDSA, D&AD, Red Dot, and more. But unlike many award-winning designs, it has also been a huge market success, with the announcement in April 2007 that the total iPod sales worldwide had reached one hundred million units since the first one was sold in November 2001.[2]

The iPod's physical design is iconic. Its minimal geometric form has been pared down to straight edges and radiused corners, complemented by a subtle choice of materials and finishes. On the fourth- and fifth-generation models, the plain front moldings were back sprayed in a carefully tinted white, seamlessly set into a stainless steel back etched with a logo and the words "Designed by Apple in California."

This attention to detail continues into the interaction design. Over successive generations of the classic iPod, the controls were distilled into a single circle, cleverly combining discrete commands and navigation. Pressing down at the cardinal points (the north, south, east, and west of the dial, as it were) triggers playing and pausing, skipping to the next or previous track, while scrolling around the wheel navigates through menus and other controls, with a button at the center to make selections. The track wheel feels beautifully direct and responsive, although not since the mechanical scroll wheel on the first-generation iPod has it actually rotated. Yet its tactility is reinforced by discreet audible clicks that you can imagine you are feeling through your fingertips. Overall, the industrial design and interaction design are beautifully integrated, conceived with respect to each other, in contrast to so many other products in which the physical design and the interface have obviously been created by different design teams.

How can it be that despite its ubiquity and many imitators, the iPod still appears so refreshingly simple? Jonathan Ive's design team at Apple is notorious for its relentless pursuit of every last detail, and the time and effort needed for even a good team to do justice to a design should not be underestimated. The iPod falls victim to its own success, being so obvious in hindsight, belying the effort that was required to achieve it. Many iterations of the design were needed to achieve this apparent lightness of touch, another manifestation of the quotation, "If I had had more time, I would have written a shorter letter."[3] Simple things are not necessarily easier to design.

Simplicity is not a style that has been applied to the final product. Behind the outward design, the whole concept is simple, right down to the original tagline, "1,000 songs in your pocket."[4] The physical design is then as much as anything an outward manifestation of this inner simplicity.

All design is subject to constraints. Constraints arise both from what the design is required to do (including user needs or desires) and how this might be achieved (usually technical feasibility or business viability). But part of the design process may be to deliberately further constrain the design brief—either narrowing its scope or limiting the complexity of the response. The Apple design team places a high value on the restraint of a specification, not just its comprehensiveness. In a rare interview with the *New York Times*, Ive said, "It was about being very focused and not trying to do too much with the device—which would have been its complication and, therefore, its demise. . . . The key was getting rid of stuff."[5]

appliances and platforms

The iPod is an example of what designers and others sometimes call an *appliance*: a product dedicated to a limited function, but to performing this really well. This is in contrast to *platforms*, which are conceived as multipurpose products, epitomized by personal digital assistants (PDAs) and palmtop personal computers that run a diversity of applications, from business spreadsheets to entertainment media players. An analogy is sometimes made to cutlery versus a Swiss Army knife: the latter is useful if your priority is to carry a single object to do many things, but few of us choose to eat with one in the privacy of our own homes. This is a discussion that is contentious and even subject to fashion; the iPod has definitely provided an icon for the appliance, whereas many cell phones are expanding into the territory of multifunction platforms. Indeed, Apple's own iPhone is advertised as a combination of three products: a cell phone, a media player (music and video

Apple iPhone

player), and an Internet device. It will be interesting to see how these trends evolve.

Whichever dominates, appliances and platforms continue to coexist because people have different tastes. Peter Bosher is a technology consultant specializing in speech and audio production, and Steve Tyler is a head of technical product development. Both are blind, but they have different aspirations for accessible products. They both use a Braille-Lite, a dedicated special needs product that lets them type and read electronic braille. Bosher would like an integrated platform that unites his Braille-Lite, PDA, and cell phone so that he would have less objects to carry around with him (although in this context, the multitouch display that gives the iPhone its flexibility is unlikely to be appropriate, since it relies on the user seeing each new manifestation of its visual interface). In contrast, Tyler would just like a simple but accessible cell phone, as elegant and attractive as any other, because he would feel more self-confident using this in public rather than a more conspicuous and overtly technical product. This is clearly not about technophilia versus technophobia, because both Bosher and Tyler are highly technically adept. It is more about personal tastes.

Neither is this about low-tech versus high-tech. Bruce Sterling, the science fiction author and writer on technology, design, and society, has identified a progression from *products*, mass-manufactured objects that broadly correspond to the appliances described above, to platforms, which Sterling calls *gizmos* and describes as "highly unstable, user-alterable, baroquely multi-featured objects, commonly programmable, with a brief lifespan."[6] He is more interested in the technosocial than the technological, and examines the demands this has placed on the people who use these objects. *Consumers* of products have been forced to become the *end users* of gizmos, spending their time as well as money on the "extensive, sustained interaction" of upgrades, plug-ins, and unsolicited messages.[7]

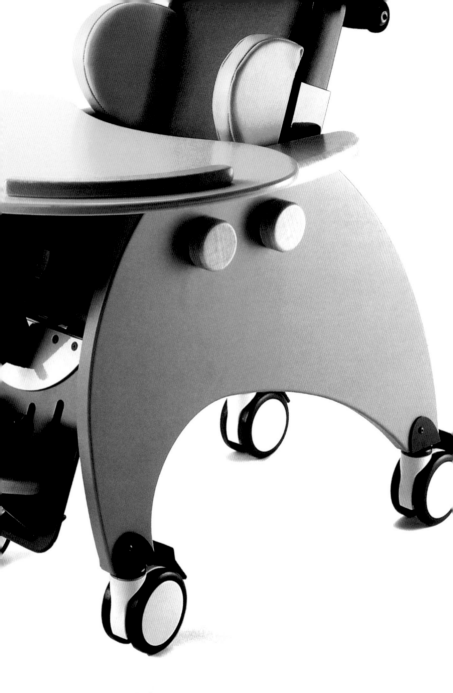

Leckey Woosh chair

Sterling anticipates the advent of what he names *spimes*, in many ways more functionally advanced than any current platform, but in many other ways more appliance-like in their focus. Spimes, he says, will be manufactured objects with a narrow primary role, yet integrated with a world of information, recording data about their entire life span, archived in case of as-yet-unforeseen ecological benefits.[8] Objects as inert and straightforward as wine bottles could all be spimes in the future, becoming physical links to the information about their own ecological footprint and that of the wine they contain.

Design has always enjoyed a provocative relationship with technology. The ethos of the postwar Royal College of Art in London, inspired by the Bauhaus, has been summarized as "attuned to new technologies, self-confident, anarchic."[9] But it is technology as a means to an end, not an end in itself. Christopher Frayling, rector of the Royal College of Art, says that one big issue with design students is that technical constraints and technical possibilities can all too often be allowed to dominate. We should be as skeptical about doing things just because they are possible as we are ambitious about achieving difficult but desirable ends. It is time to stop letting the technology "push us around," observes Frayling. "Let's bring the users in and let's bring delight back into everyday products, because it seems to have gone."[10]

the flying submarine

The preoccupations of inclusive design can mean that products with disability in mind have a greater tendency to be conceived as platforms. The principle of universal design or design for the whole population can lead to designs that are not just accessible to everyone but that also seek to accommodate everybody's needs. But this pressure also exists in design for special needs too.

James Leckey manufactures furniture for children with cerebral palsy—furniture that has won international design awards. Leckey's product range has to meet the needs of children of different ages, different sizes, and with a diversity of clinical conditions. It also needs to cater to different uses and contexts, to support children at school, in their homes, and elsewhere. As a result, there is enormous pressure to produce adjustable, versatile, *universal* solutions that accommodate the largest number of children and from a manufacturing perspective benefit from an economy of scale.

Yet Leckey has moved away from aspiring to universal solutions. Too much adjustability and modularity can result in a design that is visually complex, and that can be intimidating to the children and their friends. If one of the goals of this furniture is to enable disabled children to attend mainstream schools, then this goal is undermined if the equipment itself stigmatizes the kids among their new peers and prevents social integration. How the furniture looks and feels can be almost as important as what it does.

Leckey recognizes that these conflicting demands may be inherent in the product specification itself, and cannot always be reconciled in the design. He uses the expression *flying submarine* to represent a product overburdened with features and doomed to mediocrity in each. A machine that travels on land, water, and air sounds attractive, but we continue to prefer the inconvenience of transferring between less versatile vehicles.

In order to resist this pressure for a single product that suits everyone, everywhere, James Leckey Design has changed its entire means of production, creating instead the flexibility to build a wider range of relatively focused products. Patterns are held in computer-aided design databases, parts are individually laser-cut, and each chair is assembled to order. Within this process, making many different designs to suit different children can be almost as economical as trying to fit the children into a single design.

Leckey's in-house design team, working with Alan Marks and David Edgerley at consultants Triplicate Isis, has consistently recognized the importance of design in every aspect of the company's manufacture, service, and brand. These are common sensibilities within consumer markets, but less so within design for disability. James Leckey has been featured on the cover of *Design* magazine, which wrote that he and his company "look at cosmetic aspects; not for the sake of it, but primarily to focus on the needs of the user."[11] Simplicity in concept and simplicity of form are there for the children themselves.

simpler still

Returning to Apple, the iPod shuffle represents a further distillation of Apple's principles. When the possibility of a much smaller music player arose, rather than opt for a smaller display and a compromised version of the iPod interface, Apple courageously dispensed with a display altogether. With it, Apple relinquished the functionality that might depend on one, so the iPod shuffle does not allow the user to select individual tracks or even view the names of the tracks. It pares down the iPod interface to a product that gives the user just two choices: either playing the tracks in the order they were downloaded, or shuffling them into a random order.

The iPod shuffle challenges the notion that products always get more complex as they evolve because more and more features are added, either because this becomes technically possible or else someone asks for them. This is the antithesis of focus group–led product development that so often seems to result in ballooning functionality. After all, if people are asked whether they might like a feature, why shouldn't they say "yes"? Early on in the design process, the designers are the ones who usually have a feeling for what might be lost by incorporating more and more, and what might be gained

Apple iPod and iPod shuffle

by keeping things simpler. Whereas within the technical and clinical teams that are often pioneering design for disability, it is not universally acknowledged that designers or design even have a role to play at this stage of the process. Design is frequently seen as a downstream activity, even an optional one. "Most people make the mistake of thinking design is what it looks like," Apple chief executive officer Steve Jobs told the New York Times. "That's not what we think design is. It's not just what it looks like and feels like. Design is how it works."[12]

Apple represents a challenging combination of the two cultures we have considered: Jobs's vision of "the computer for the rest of us" is fundamentally inclusive in spirit.[13] Yet is Apple's design process wholly democratic, or might there be said to be a hint of benevolent design dictatorship about it? In its very conception as much as its realization, the iPod shuffle epitomizes the sensibilities of the designer. Setting the brief does not precede the design process; it is a fundamental part of the design process. Sometimes the most creative act of all is to provocatively constrain the specification.

audible media

For products designed to play media, it is interesting to compare the accessibility of the product with that of the medium itself. The user interface on the iPod shuffle has been pared down to tactile buttons: it is essentially nonvisual. In this way the music, the thing we are interested in, is accessible to many people with visual impairments. Of course, the whole picture is more complicated and complex; visual impairment does not preclude dexterity, hearing, or cognitive impairment, and the iPod interface extends to the personal computer, which allows the mobile functionality to be so simple. But the interaction design and the medium nevertheless seem somehow in tune.

Contrast this with the recent evolution of radios: because the Digital Audio Broadcasting standard supports text streams in parallel with the audio content, text displays have been added to most radios. Is this an innocuous step? Well, once added, these displays are usually employed for the main user interface as well, replacing direct tuning dials with a more generic menu structure with lists that may change depending on which stations are available, and thus cannot be memorized. The result can be radios that have become less easy to use for visually impaired people. While it is important not to overstate this irony—the provocative website BlindKiss.com, of which more in a later chapter, lists "Ten Things Not to Say to a Blind Person," including "Radio must be really important to you"—the irony stands.

A common remedy is to adopt a multimedia approach, adding a deliberate redundancy of channels of information and feedback, such as an audible click to a button press that might not be felt, or a flashing beacon to a siren that might not be heard. In the case of Digital Audio Broadcasting radios, one obvious approach would be to add text-to-speech to the visual text display. Why does this remind me of the children's cautionary tale "There was an old lady who swallowed a fly. . . . She swallowed a spider to catch the fly" (and so on)? Tyler, head of technical product development at the RNIB, has learned from experience that multimodal interfaces are often pursued for their own sake. One video recorder launched with a so-called talking user interface was in fact as inaccessible as any other one. Speech technology had been added in order to differentiate the product in an overcrowded marketplace— just because it *could* be added, not because of *why* it should have been.

I believe that more thought could go into improving accessibility by simplifying an interface, not always augmenting it. Radio is still fundamentally an auditory medium. What if a radio's user interface were once again auditory, as it used to be when tuning with a simple dial? Then, at least the accessibility of the interface would match the accessibility of the medium itself. It could even be said to celebrate the medium. Beyond accessibility, should our experiences of different media necessarily converge? I'll discuss this further in the next chapter.

simple radios

But there are other reasons for designing simple radios. The Bath Institute of Medical Engineering (BIME) is an organization that has been developing products for and with disabled people for many years. Recently, it has been exploring the use of technology within the homes of people with dementia. As radios have become more complicated, they also have become more difficult to use, especially for people with dementia. BIME has resorted to repackaging a radio, leaving just the on/ off switch visible and hiding the other controls away so that the user cannot inadvertently retune.

With a different agenda, students in the Innovative Product Design degree program at the University of Dundee have also designed single-station radios—iconic radios that reflect the content of a particular radio station. For their tutors Jon Rogers and Polly Duplock, this blurring of industrial design and interaction design is about connecting product, medium, and service.

On the front of the BIME radio, so that people know what it is, the word "Radio" is written in large letters. But a radio can also be made more or less obviously a radio through its form and materials, rather than by labeling it. Revisiting historical forms and archetypes may be particularly appropriate, as dementia can leave longer-term memories relatively intact. The preoccupations of the Milan furniture fair seem relevant: identifying and distilling the essence of a chair, a light, or in this case a radio. Designers would be inspired to work in this territory as well as having valuable perspectives and skills to contribute. And simple iconic radios could also have mainstream appeal, as manufactured by Tivoli Audio and others.

simplified radio by the Bath Institute of Medical Engineering

The head of BIME, Roger Orpwood, explains that dementia is often accompanied by a heightened artistic appreciation and emotional response. So it is likely that the beauty of the objects around individuals with dementia, both everyday objects and those designed for them, could play a part in people's experiences of living with this condition. In other words, design values are every bit as relevant as they would be in any other area of design, and perhaps even more so.

without thought

The themes of simplicity and accessibility recombine again in a piece that defines a cutting edge of design and also suggests provocative new directions for inclusive design. A wall-mounted CD player, designed by Naoto Fukasawa and manufactured by Muji, was not conceived to be accessible in the conventional sense, but nonetheless is a highly inclusive product. The designer's philosophy was to produce a product that could be used *without thought*—a theme that Fukasawa has explored in workshops and exhibitions. He is interested in objects that tap into a general cultural consciousness, not just the recent history of electronic products.

This CD player can be used without thinking because it alludes to an old-fashioned electric ventilation fan, a relatively traditional object that most people will have come across or else can intuitively guess how to use. A circular, CD-size depression on the front surface indicates that a disc be placed directly on to the spindle at the center. It is then natural to reach for the only visible control: a cord hanging down that has a light-switch pull on it, inviting it to be pulled. A tug on the cord sets the disc visibly spinning; another tug stops it again.

This simplicity supports cognitive inclusion, otherwise one of the most difficult and least understood challenges facing inclusive design. But the same simplicity comes at a cost: there is no display to tell the listener the name of the track

Muji CD player designed by Naoto Fukasawa

being played or how long it will last. There is no treble or bass enhancement, just a knurled volume control that can be felt protruding from the top surface (and as a further concession to control, forward and reverse buttons are hidden on the top surface, but these begin to feel like a bit of a compromise).

It is only this degree of simplicity that allows the design as a whole to communicate the purpose and use of the product—something impossible if either are too complex. Furthermore it creates a truly iconic presence. The design language is its essence, not just something applied, and there is a quiet humor and wit behind it all.

The result is arguably a highly accessible product, but certainly not a universal design in the sense of incorporating all the functionality that every user might have wished for. Consumers balance the qualities of any product, however, and many have decided that the reduction in features, if indeed this isn't an advantage in itself, is worth the simple delight. The whole exceeds the sum of the parts.

aspiring to a lightness of touch

Good design often requires the courage to value simplicity over being "all things to all people."[14] This might conflict with some definitions of universal design, yet at the same time it can actually make a design more accessible because simple products are often the most cognitively and culturally inclusive.

Cognitive accessibility is frequently overlooked, perhaps because it is more difficult to quantify than is accessibility on the basis of sight or hearing, dexterity or mobility. The danger of adding flexibility and complexity to achieve accessibility is that a product may become difficult to learn how to use in any of its different ways. It may be inclusive in principle, but not in practice.

Experienced designers develop a feel for the relationship between *in principle* and *in practice*, between the design brief and the design response, and most important, between the parts and the whole. Sometimes it is better to deny the user a feature that could have been useful, in favor of a better overall experience. This is why setting the brief in the first place is a fundamental part of the design process, and why designers as well as users should be at the heart of any team from the start.

There still remains the possibility that with products and services, unlike buildings, design for the whole population might be achieved through a diversity of alternatives, each inclusive in different ways, yet still fairly limited in complexity. This discussion is continued in the next chapter.

identity meets ability

Alan Newell, Sebastien Sablé, Amar Latif, Steve Tyler, Crispin Jones
Antony Rabin, and Jamie Buchanan
Silen-T watch and The Discretion Watch, WHO and IDEO
voice PDA and BlindStation, RNIB and RNID, deaf and Deaf
eavesdropping hearing aids and Cat's ears, acoustic throne and Table Talk

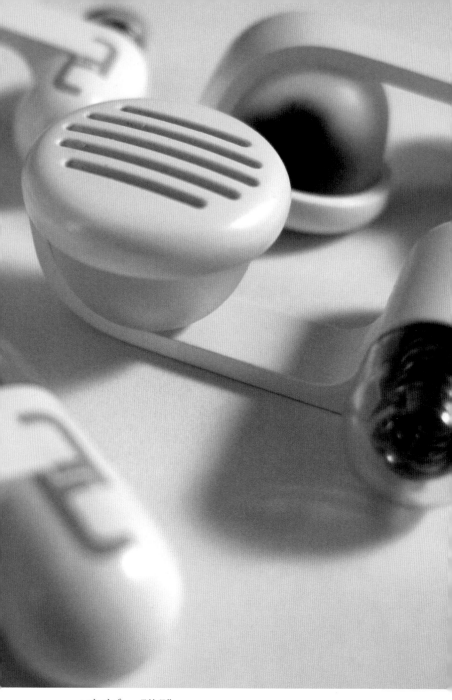

earbuds from *Table Talk*

ability

When designing for disabled people there is a tendency to focus on ability and disability. A distinction is sometimes made between a supposedly negative emphasis on disability and an affirming emphasis on ability, but in either case the issue of ability can dominate.

So the user group for any design for special needs is usually described in terms of a particular impairment that they share, and the penetration of inclusive design is generally discussed in terms of the number of people in the population within the ranges of abilities accommodated. From this perspective, the market is being defined and divided primarily along the lines of ability.

Over the last few decades, definitions of disability have become broader and more sophisticated. The World Health Organization (WHO) acknowledges that every human being can experience some degree of disability.[1] Its definitions, which will be further discussed below, blur the boundaries between disabled and so-called able-bodied people.

But in the same document, the WHO's own definitions of "general products and technology" and "assistive products and technology" remain quite distinct. Perhaps it is time to do more to blur the boundaries between mainstream design and design for disability? Perhaps this involves challenging the distinction between universal design and design for special needs?

identity

Inappropriately defining people in terms of their ability also runs the risk of stereotyping populations of people who share a particular disability, but may otherwise be as diverse as the population as a whole. A shared disability does not preclude a diversity of culture, tastes, wealth, temperament, education, values, attitudes, and priorities.

Traditionally, design for disability has paid more attention to the clinical than the cultural diversity within any group. The same prostheses, wheelchairs, and communication devices are often offered to people with a particular disability, whether they are seventeen or seventy years old, and regardless of their attitudes, toward their disability or otherwise. And does inclusive design, in its aspiration to be universal, risk stereotyping everybody?

Meanwhile, mainstream design, whatever its other shortcomings, is devoting more effort to a richer understanding of people. *User-centered design* is broadening from traditional physical ergonomics into cultural diversity and individual identity. Design ethnography and other qualitative design research methods are increasingly used within education, industry, and business.

tension

Bringing a richer sense of identity into design for disability would involve more than just introducing design ethnography, however. And its implications would be more profound and contentious: understanding for whom we are designing acknowledges that we are not designing for everybody at once. Might that seem divisive in a market traditionally doing its best to cater to everyone's unmet needs? Or is this inherent in the wider move from a medical to a social model of disability?

This could fragment existing markets—or allow them to fragment; perhaps a market defined by ability alone is rather contrived in the first place. At the same time, being more sensitive to identity might open up new paths to mainstream markets, where consumers expect this perspective. This chapter will challenge traditional markets for design for disability, using examples from visual impairment and hearing impairment. Since most of the examples are taken from my own experience, they are illustrative rather than definitive. In the case of visual impairment, they explore a blurring of the boundaries between design for disability and ability; in the case of hearing impairment, they illustrate a sharpening of the definitions of identity.

contextual disability

This book is not seeking to redefine disability, but a brief look at some of the existing definitions is appropriate. The WHO's *International Classification of Functioning, Disability, and Health* (ICF) recognizes disability as a complex interaction between the features of a person's body and the features of the environment and society in which that person lives.[2] It makes a distinction between an "impairment": a problem in a body function or structure; an "activity limitation": a difficulty encountered in executing a task; and a "participation restriction": a problem experienced in involvement in life situations. In the WHO's words, "Disability is not something that only happens to a minority of humanity. The ICF thus 'mainstreams' the experience of disability and recognizes it as a universal human experience."[3]

The inclusion of *contextual factors* challenges a direct causal relationship from *impairment* to *disability* to *handicap* that other definitions had embodied. It speaks of blurring the boundaries between disabled and able-bodied, not just in terms of a gray scale or continuum between the two, but also because changing environmental factors and social contexts make disability contextual, even dynamic, for each individual.

resonance of needs

Taking a broader view still (even if this departs from accepted definitions), contextual factors and activity restrictions might be said to also affect people who might not be classified as being disabled. Defining anybody as disabled or able-bodied somehow implies that this is a constant: that each of us is either always *disabled* or always *able-bodied*. Yet our abilities change depending on the context. Environments themselves may render us more or less capable, but so may activities or states of mind. If we already have our hands full, our ability to carry out a task demanding dexterity is affected; if we are preoccupied by one thing, our ability to see something else may be compromised; if we are tired, distracted, upset, or unable to speak a local language, we may acquire at least the symptoms of a reduced cognitive ability. Alan Newell, who has for several decades researched accessibility and aging, engages his students at the University of Dundee with the thought that all of these abilities may be subject to alcohol-related impairment.[4]

This view seeds the idea that particular disabled and nondisabled people may nonetheless have shared needs in particular circumstances, despite their differing abilities at other times. And of course, particular disabled and nondisabled people may have shared tastes and priorities that have nothing at all to do with their abilities.

resonant design

While blurring the boundaries between disability and ability, at the same time the *International Classification of Functioning, Disability, and Health* maintains a clear distinction between design for disability and mainstream design. It defines assistive products and technology as "adapted or specially designed equipment, products and technologies that assist people in daily living, such as prosthetic and orthotic devices, neural prostheses (e.g., functional stimulation devices that control bowels, bladder, breathing and heart rate), and environmental control units aimed at facilitating individuals' control over their indoor settings (scanners, remote control systems, voice-controlled systems, timer switches)."[5]

On the other hand, it defines general products and technology as "equipment, products and technologies used by people in daily activities, such as clothes, textiles, furniture, appliances, cleaning products and tools, not adapted or specially designed."[6] This comfortably accommodates universal design, which challenges the notion that accessibility need involve anything being *specially designed*, because this should be the default.

There seems to be a yawning gap between the two definitions, between the medical language of the former and the qualification that the latter not be specially designed. This perpetuates a separation between medical engineering and design in general, whatever the WHO's wish to "mainstream" disability. But perhaps it is not for the WHO but the design community to challenge this distinction.

I would like to propose the term *resonant design* for a design intended to address the needs of some people with a particular disability and other people without that disability but perhaps finding themselves in particular circumstances. So this is neither design just for able-bodied people nor design for the whole population; nor even does it assume that everyone with a particular disability will have the same needs. It is something between these extremes, not as a compromise, but as a fundamental aspiration.

To appeal to both groups, such design would also need to embody the design quality that a mainstream market demands.

As examples of resonant design, here are just three themes, design briefs, ideas, or products that involve resonance between the needs of *some* people with visual impairment and those of *some* people without. The shared need, the *resonance*, is quite different in each case. Designing for people with visual impairment is thought provoking because design is often narrowly considered to be a visual medium. Does design have a role? Furthermore, visually impaired and sighted people will clearly have different experiences of a design that suits them both, so both perspectives must be considered.

visual impairment and expertise

The consultancy IDEO is perhaps still best known for having designed the Palm V, a palmtop computer or PDA.[7] Years later, this attracted a German start-up company that was developing speech technology to invite IDEO to help it design a voice-enabled PDA. At that time, getting voice recognition and synthetic speech onto a portable device was pioneering, and while this venture did not progress into production, its early steps were an exercise in resonant design.

The primary users were to be busy professionals who might benefit from the eyes-free use of a PDA in circumstances where interaction through a small screen and a stylus would be inappropriate, such as traveling businesspeople, warehouse managers, or architects on-site. The client had already recognized a common need with visually impaired people, between people who wanted eyes-free interaction in particular circumstances and those who depended on it. And the client saw this as a significant secondary market, given the millions of visually impaired people across Europe alone.

So that this market was not treated as an afterthought, we recruited two visually impaired people into the design team. So often a product or service is accessible in principle, but let down by a fundamental flaw, based on an oversight or a misconception of an able-bodied design team.

This collaboration, though, was not simply an exercise in accessibility but also in mutual benefit, in order to design a better product for everyone. Our visually impaired people were already expert users of nonvisual user interfaces, and their years of using screen readers and other technologies gave them invaluable insights that we may never have uncovered in short-term user testing. For example, they knew from experience how important it was to be able to change the rate of synthetic speech; as novices they had needed speech at normal conversational rates, but as experts quickly found this excruciatingly slow and frustrating. Navigating a user interface is not the same as having a conversation, and experts will increase the speed to a rate that a novice finds unintelligible.

So by involving expert visually impaired people we would design a better product for future sighted experts too. Resonance of needs can be approached from either direction, from sighted to visually impaired or vice versa.

visual impairment and audiophilia

It is possible to become overwhelmed by issues of ability and accessibility to the exclusion of all others. This can risk missing resonances that have less to do with need than with personal taste. Audiobooks may have been first introduced as *books on tape* for visually impaired people, yet now represent an even larger mainstream market.[8] Many people who can read printed books enjoy the alternative experience of hearing a book read to them. The qualities of the reading are important, as they are for visually impaired people too, and critics review new recordings in the weekend newspapers, alongside traditional book reviews.

Millions of listeners still tune into their radios not because they are visually impaired or wish to occupy their eyes with some other task but because they enjoy the medium of radio. So there are several reasons for designing a digital radio with no visual display at all: to make it accessible to visually impaired people, to allow people to drift off to sleep listening to the radio, changing stations in the dark or with their eyes closed, or just to celebrate the unique qualities of this nonvisual medium. Our interactions with electronic products, from televisions to washing machines, hi-fis to vending machines, are converging toward screen-based user interfaces. Leaving aside that exclusion can be locked into these conventions, this also precludes the satisfying *hand-ear* coordination demanded of older radio dials. This simple interaction may have been a less efficient means of finding a known station, but allowed browsing, as the listener gleans content from the short snippets of audio, and stumbles across programs or stations they didn't know were there. The concentration required to find a signal, analogous to safecracking, immerses the listener in the medium itself, rather than separates them from it. The rewards can justify the increased demands.

Increasing the level of interactivity further, researcher Sebastien Sablé has been developing BlindStation, an audio

Tissot Silen-T tactile watch

game platform adapted to the needs of visually impaired children.[9] It would be interesting to look for resonance with sighted children traveling to school by bus who may wish to play a game, but at the same time watch the world go by—an interesting alternative to mobile games that seek to create immersive visual experiences sometimes beyond the capabilities of their tiny screens. What games already exist that can be played without looking? What new games might be conceived? If Sablé succeeds in a game that is addictive for visually impaired kids, then sighted kids will probably be attracted too. Conversely, if it does not appeal to sighted players, then is it of a quality that visually impaired people deserve?

visual impairment and discretion

For visually impaired people who cannot read the dial of a wristwatch, special watches are available. Some are tactile, analogue watches with hands that are robust enough for the wearer to feel their position, otherwise protected from damage by a folding cover. These are usually old-fashioned in appearance and poorly visually designed. Others are electronic *talking watches* that use a speech synthesizer to speak the time, and tend to have the appearance of cheap digital watches. Visually impaired people are not offered the quality, choice, or potential for self-expression that many sighted people enjoy now that watches are considered as much fashion accessories as functional timekeepers.

An exception is the Silen-T watch, developed by Swiss manufacturer Tissot with the involvement of the RNIB. Tissot had developed a watch face that responded like a touch screen, and employed this in rugged watches for outdoor pursuits to select stopwatch, altimeter, and compass functions without the need for vulnerable buttons. In the Silen-T watches, this touch screen technology is combined with vibration, creating a watch that can be read by touch. The wearers run a finger around the edge of the face, which responds by vibrating

scenario for *The Discretion Watch* by Crispin Jones

when the finger is over one of the watch hands—one vibration pattern for the hour hand, and another for the minute hand. This means that visually impaired people can tell the time by touch, for once in a mainstream product that is mass-produced and available in mainstream shops.

"The engineers paid a lot of attention to quality and finish," says Tyler, head of technical product development at the RNIB, "applying the same standards as to any of their watches."[10] All this attention comes at a price, but Tyler is adamant that products for people with disabilities should not always be designed down to a minimum cost. He'd like there to be a choice of accessible watches from a tactile Swatch to a tactile Rolex—not to everyone's tastes, but shouldn't that be for the wearer to decide? Amar Latif, who is also visually impaired and the founder of the Traveleyes travel company, is one of the sharpest dressers I know.

Tissot didn't conceive of the Silen-T being just for visually impaired people, however. For sighted people, the Silen-T is a rugged watch with a vibrating alarm function, which in some circumstances can be more noticeable than an audible alarm and is also useful to hearing impaired people. In the same way that people set their cell phones to *silent*, it can also be more discreet. As Tissot expresses it in the user's manual, "This function enables every individual wearer to tell the time very discreetly, and offers particular benefits to visually impaired people for whom this watch represents a long awaited step forward."[11]

The issue of discretion could be taken further. Artist and designer Crispin Jones and I collaborated on the design of a related but more experimental watch, inspired by the mutual interests of visually impaired and sighted people.[12] While a visually impaired person may be unable to read a watch, a sighted person may be reluctant to look at hers for fear of offending the people in her company by indicating boredom.

This brings the history of the tactile watch full circle. In 1795, watchmaker Abraham Louis Breguet made a watch that

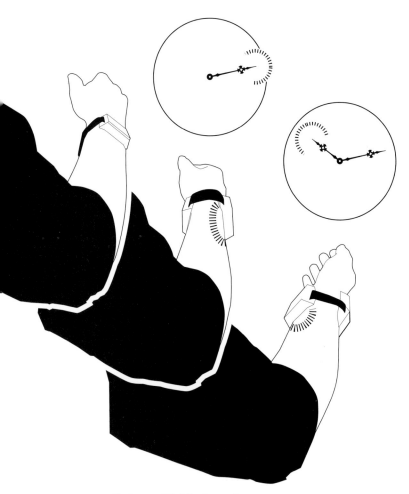

using *The Discretion Watch* by Crispin Jones

could be read by touch. This beautiful watch had a hand that could be turned until it met resistance, with the time given by the position of this resistance in relation to small bumps around the rim representing the hours. "In the late eighteenth century it was considered impolite to consult one's watch in company, a question of etiquette which the *à tact* watch helped to solve (the French tact, meaning touch, has given the English tact and tactful)," and this history goes on to record that "this kind of tactile watch is now mainly used by the blind and visually impaired."[13]

Here is a resonance of needs where unfortunately a talking watch would be more blatant than a standard watch. Even a tactile watch might alert suspicion as the wearer interrogated it with his other hand. Instead, *The Discretion Watch* can be read without even touching it with the other hand. When the wearer rotates his forearm at the wrist, they will feel vibrations in certain orientations. This allows the wearer to feel the time in response to languid and, with practice, indecipherable body movements.

In these few examples of resonance between the needs of some people with visual impairment and other people without, the mutual interests are as much about identity as ability. Issues of identity can be just as profound and inspiring.

Disabled with a capital D; disability with a little d

Just as our diverse abilities are recognized, so diversity should be acknowledged within any disability, whereas people with the same disability are still often stereotyped as a homogeneous group. Tyler says that even the RNIB is moving away from a philosophy of *design for all*, and becoming more considered about when to advocate a single universal solution for all visually impaired people and when to advocate a choice between complementary alternatives.

When IDEO was researching a project with RNID (the Hear-Wear project described in **fashion meets discretion**), conversations with hard of hearing people exposed different experiences of deafness. When Antony Rabin, who has been deaf since birth, first mentioned that he was "Deaf with a capital D," we took him to mean that he was very deaf indeed: profoundly deaf. But when he repeated the expression, we asked him what he meant by it. He explained that for many people, their deafness is a large part of their cultural identity. In adulthood, most of his close friends are deaf and use sign language, so they have a shared experience. Therefore he chooses to define himself as *Deaf with a capital D*. Many deaf people feel so strongly about this aspect of their identity, that while they may wear hearing aids, they are ambivalent about future medical or technical developments that could give them permanent hearing. Their deafness is not something to be cured but an integral part of them. Understandably, they can have mixed feelings about whether their children might inherit their deafness or be born hearing.

In contrast, people that are defined as *deaf with a little d* may not even recognize a Deaf/deaf distinction themselves. They are more likely to have been brought up within a hearing family and school, and may be more skilled at lip-reading, but hearing impairment is still a barrier to interaction with their hearing friends and colleagues. Deaf with a little d is probably how most of us without a hearing impairment would imagine an acquired hearing impairment would affect us. For this group of people, deafness is a source of social isolation more than belonging, and any opportunity of improved hearing is less of a dilemma. The role of technology and medical science is different; so, then, might the role of design be.

The big D/little d cultural divide is clearly a fundamental segmentation of a hearing loss market, cutting across gender, age, or occupation. Similar divisions can apply to other disabilities, and the extent to which individuals chose to define themselves in terms or in spite of their disabilities. Could it even be an argument against universal design? Inclusive design aspires to remove barriers based on ability. Yet behind these barriers may lie other cultural divisions that should not necessarily be dismantled in turn but perhaps respected and left intact.

On this particular project, we were looking for resonances between the needs of deaf/hard of hearing and hearing people that could inspire early design concepts. It seems appropriate that one concept was inspired by a Deaf with a capital D person, and one by a deaf with a little d person. And while both concepts may have appealed to different mainstream markets, each may not have suited the other hearing impaired user. Neither is aiming to be universal.

tuning in; tuning out

The first concept, inspired by our conversation with a Deaf with a capital D individual, considered his ambivalent relationship with his residual hearing and his hearing aids. One thing he valued about his hearing aids was their versatility: he could use them to vary his hearing ability from nonhearing to superhuman. He can choose to be nonhearing in an art gallery, where if children are running around and other people are talking, he tends to remove his hearing aids altogether and enjoy immersing himself in the paintings in silence. He is superhuman in the office, where he has discovered that if he walks down a corridor and switches his hearing aid to the T setting, to receive signals from induction loops, he can pick up the conversation in a conference room on the floor above and eavesdrop on a meeting he hasn't been invited to.

This ability to vary ones hearing could appeal to hearing people too, and a pair of hearing aids offering a choice of superhuman hearing or no hearing at all might be developed with wider appeal. It could be fascinating to tune in to an unheard urban soundscape of leaky induction loops, a new psychogeographic channel. At other times, it could be preferable to tune out the noise pollution in which silence and the privacy that it can bring are increasingly rare commodities. We

earbud from *Table Talk* designed by IDEO for RNID HearWear project called this concept *cat's ears*, with reference to a domestic cat's impressively sensitive yet selective hearing. It then became a moral dilemma whether they should signal their current state, perhaps through the opening or closing of visible irises, or whether an observer should be left unsettled by not knowing whether they were being listened to or not.

Table Talk

A very different concept arose from our experience of speaking with Jamie Buchanan, someone who we realized in hindsight was deaf with a little d. He, industrial designer Caroline Flagiello, and I had each spent our mornings in an office, and we decided to adjourn to a coffeehouse for a change of scene. We sat down with our drinks, but when we tried to continue our discussion, we found that we couldn't hear each other above the hiss of the espresso machine, the clatter of crockery, and the buzz of nearby conversations. This affected all of us, hearing and hard of hearing alike. So we asked for our coffees to be decanted into paper cups and retreated to the silence of the office again.

A silent coffeehouse would not have been the solution to our problem, because the noise was part of the ambience and vibrancy that had attracted us in the first place. Jamie explained that bars and cafés present a dilemma to hearing impaired people. Whether or not they wear hearing aids, background noise can make it difficult to discriminate speech. For those relying on lip-reading, as the conversation changes hands spontaneously around a table, the lip-reader needs to look from person to person to follow the speech. "I'm always playing catch-up, trying to work out what each person is saying, having missed their first few words," explained Jamie. Ultimately, these difficulties can lead to a reluctance to visit these venues and an increased social isolation.

From a social perspective, hearing impairment is something that affects a group of friends, not just an individual, and a

detail of copper induction loop in tabletop from *Table Talk*

conversation, not just one side of it. So despite the prevalence of the miniaturization and personalization of technology, perhaps designing a portable or wearable device is not the most interesting response. Hearing loss could be seen as a symptom of a whole environment, so maybe it could be addressed at this scale.

These days *hearing technology* conjures up miniature, in-ear devices, perhaps wirelessly networked to other mobile products. A lineage could be traced from handheld ear trumpets, via early electronic body-worn hearing aids and further miniaturization, to current digital in-the-ear hearing aids— changing technologies, but the same basic concept. But some early hearing aids were conceived on a much larger scale. In the early nineteenth century, King John VI of Portugal commissioned an acoustic throne. His subjects knelt and spoke into lions' mouths carved into the arms of the throne, and the sound was channeled through acoustic cavities inside the chair to emerge from vents by his ears. The ritual of subjugation was as important as the sound quality. The Victorians invented perforated urns that could be placed on a table in the center of a room, with a rubber tube connected to an earpiece. The urn was better positioned than the hard of hearing host to pick up sound equally from everyone in the room. The early history of hearing technology, as with many other technologies, contains some approaches that would be radical again today. Working at a different scale can open up quite different possibilities. Conceiving of hearing technology as an environment or furniture, rather than a personal device, provokes new thoughts.

The concept that emerged supports conversation for a whole group, not just an individual. *Table Talk* is a combination of furniture and earpieces.[14] People sit around tables that are wired with microphones on each edge, fed into inductive loops on the opposite side. This is just the same induction loop system technology routinely used at bank tellers' windows and in cinemas.

Anyone wearing a hearing aid is already equipped to benefit from this environment, which will help to distinguish speech across the table from ambient background noise. It is the rest of us who would need special earpieces to pick up these signals too. These simple earpieces would not require their own microphone and would be less likely to suffer from feedback as the distance from microphone to earpiece is greater, which is where a lot of the cost of bespoke hearing aids comes from, so they could be low-tech and low cost, even sold in blister packs behind the bar.

The design extended to the signage on the door, advertising *Table Talk* to passersby. Current T-loop signs employ the iconography of disability—an ear with a line through it representing hearing impairment. The identity created for *Table Talk* emphasized the positive experience of conversation rather than the negative experience of deafness. This is not just a euphemism: the signage should celebrate the buzz audible at the front door, not apologize for it. A concept video celebrated a noisy environment, rooted in a particular urban culture that may not be to everyone's tastes.

Table Talk sought to turn inclusive design on its head, creating an environment that initially puts hearing aid wearers at an unfair advantage, but allows others to catch up.

blurring boundaries, but sharpening focus

A dual approach of blurring and sharpening could redefine design for disability and its relationship to mainstream design. Transcending disability could cut both ways, by not necessarily broadening toward universal design, but acknowledging the diversity among people who happen to share the same impairments. Some of this diversity mirrors the dimensions of mainstream markets: age, sex, occupation, and so on. But added to this are different relationships between an individual's identity and his disability. Design has a part to play in this complex issue that is both influenced by and yet can also influence social attitudes toward disability.

Focusing on particular cultures is a goal in itself to produce appropriate designs, but it can also be a means to an end: initially designing for narrower subcultures might catalyze radical new approaches—approaches that might subsequently have more widespread applications.

The boundary between inclusive design and mainstream design is always blurred and moving. Seeking a resonance between the needs of some people with a particular disability and some people without could also blur the boundary between design for special needs and mainstream design. Exciting opportunities could exist on this frontier of resonant design.

provocative meets sensitive

Marc Quinn, Alison Lapper, Freddie Robins, Catherine Long, Mat Fraser
Anthony Dunne, Fiona Raby, Kelly Dobson
Crispin Jones, and Damon Rose
Venus de Milo and Hand of God
meat eating products and socially responsible phones
Scream Body and BlindKiss, The Electric Shock Mobile and new supersafe products

Alison Lapper Pregnant by Marc Quinn on Trafalgar Square's vacant plinth

sensitive

Design for disability has traditionally sought to avoid drawing any further unwelcome attention to the disabilities it addresses by trying to be discreet and uncontroversial, unseen or at least not remarked on. Disability can still be a source of discrimination and stigma for many disabled people, whereas a minority of medical engineers and designers are disabled themselves. Designing for and with people whose experiences they will probably never share can heighten the sensitivity toward inadvertently causing offense. But is tact the only manifestation of sensitivity?

provocative

On the other hand, there is an increasing recognition that controversy can be employed to challenge and change attitudes. There is a strong tradition of confrontational political campaigning across the disability rights movement.

In the visual arts, controversial works not only challenge our preconceptions of what constitutes art but also illuminate and expose our attitudes toward broader social issues. Within industry, design is increasingly valued not necessarily for solving problems but also for making issues visible and tangible, thereby facilitating discussion and decision making.

Meanwhile, in design research, an emerging approach of *critical design* is provoking public debate about the social and ethical implications of new technologies, rather than attempting to provide solutions. It has already been applied to many profound social issues, from the ethics of biotechnology to privacy in an age of wireless communication. Surely issues related to disability are important enough to merit applying critical design to them?

Hand of Good, Hand of God by Freddie Robins

tension

Critical design can supply a healthy challenge to the current interests and tacit values of mainstream business. But in design for disability, helping to change attitudes may be seen as less of a priority. In a field where so many everyday needs go unmet, the idea of design that does not provide direct solutions may seem wasteful and self-indulgent. How could critical design ever be justified?

Furthermore, as will become clear, critical design often relies on being uncomfortable or employing a dark humor. These might sound like inappropriate tools to bring to bear on the sensitive issues around disability. There is a tension between being sensitive to the frequently negative perceptions of people with disabilities, yet taking disability seriously enough to challenge ingrained opinions. How can these objections be countered?

This chapter will start by considering the role of art and craft in challenging attitudes toward disability. It will then introduce critical design in more depth, and explore its potential value and possible inappropriateness. Finally, a role for critical design will be established after all, through the ways in which disabled people are already challenging attitudes that they find unacceptable.

art, disability, and controversy

In contemporary Western society, we recognize that one of the roles of art is to confront and challenge our preconceptions. In 2005, an eleven-ton Carrara marble sculpture was unveiled in Trafalgar Square in London, for eighteen months occupying the vacant fourth plinth, originally intended for an equestrian statue, but never filled.[1] From its scale and setting the subject might be expected to be historical, military, and male, like its neighbors, rather than a living, pregnant, disabled woman artist.

Catherine Long wears *At One* by Freddie Robins

Alison Lapper, who says she hates the phrase "severely disabled," has phocomelia, a condition that resulted in her being born with no arms and shortened legs.[2] The sculptor was Marc Quinn, an artist previously best known for *Self*, a frozen cast of his own head in nine pints of his own blood. Quinn intended *Alison Lapper Pregnant* to be another controversial piece that would work on the viewer's subconscious "as if someone has come into your room when you're not there and moved the bed." Before its unveiling, reviewer Rachel Cooke feared that she would find the work "too deliberately controversial, too feebly didactic and, as a result, rather banal."[3] Yet on seeing the finished sculpture she was struck by "its elegant proportions, the implacable rightness of the way his subject sits there. It brings to mind the classical statues that grace our greatest museums, other sculptures from other times which also have, whether by accident or design, missing arms and legs."[4]

In her own work, Lapper has created photographic self-portraits inspired by references and contradictions between her body and the *Venus de Milo*.[5] She has mixed feelings about her early contact with medical engineering in the 1970s, with the "brown-coated, mechanical-engineering wizards in the [artificial limb] workshop" who were "less prejudiced about us than most people. We were not a blight on normal society to them, more like a physics problem that could be solved by the correct use of Newton's laws and the right raw materials. It was all very admirable but the final results, the awkward arm substitutes, were ridiculous."[6] Since then Lapper has rejected these designed prostheses. She has chosen to change her and others' attitudes toward her disability through art, not design. The artworks of Lapper and Quinn manage to be provocative and sensitive, and in being both exert a positive influence on social attitudes toward disability.

adorn equip

8th September - 18th October 2001

The City Gallery 90 Granby Street, Leicester LE1 5DJ
Opening Times : Tuesday - Friday 11.00am - 6.00pm Saturday 10.00am - 5.00pm
Telephone : 0116 254 0595 Facsimile : 0116 254 0593

A National Touring Exhibition Originated by The City Gallery, Leicester
This project has been financially supported by East Midlands Arts through the Regional Arts Lottery Programme

'Short Armed and Dangerous' Freddie Robins in consultation with Mat Fraser Machine Knitted Wool

Mat Fraser wears *Short Armed and Dangerous* by Freddie Robins

cozy attitude

Another interesting exploration of disability is to be found on the boundaries between art and design, where everyday objects are being created, but as exhibits rather than as products. Freddie Robins's work blurs traditional distinctions between art, craft, and design: she makes knitwear that often abstracts the human body and its relationship to clothing—particularly subversive given our perceptions of knitting as a craft that is conservative and cozy (a word Robins likes to play with). *Hand of Good, Hand of God* is a knitted glove a meter high, each finger of which is the size of an arm, a sleeve; each fingertip ends in a hand, a glove. As Dawn Ades, professor of art history and theory at the University of Essex, writes, "In the imagination this could be endlessly repeated enlarged or in miniature." It is an exploration of beauty and the abstraction of the body.[7]

This work is complemented by projects that have come from the other direction, in a sense: Robins has designed clothing for and with people with disabilities as part of an exhibition called *Adorn, Equip. At One* for Catherine Long, who has one arm, is a sensitive piece that acknowledges Long's body and adorns her left shoulder. It is inspiring to see Robins search for a new visual language appropriate to a body that is different; her work is neither an attempt to deny this difference nor a purely so-called functional approach. Clothing has a social and emotional function—influencing how others see us and how we feel about ourselves—that demands this perspective. Long looks comfortable in her garment and with herself, but without this being too cozy.

The actor Mat Fraser, whose body was affected by the drug Thalidomide, collaborated with Robins on another piece called *Short Armed and Dangerous*. These words are knitted into the front of the garment, a reference to Fraser's disability but more important his identity. He is photographed staring directly into the camera, the confrontational attitude he often adopts in his comedy.

meat eating products by Dunne & Raby in the Energy Gallery of the
Science Museum, London

Another collaborator on this exhibition, Ju Gosling, whose website My Not-So-Secret Life as a Cyborg had also been shown, wrote "Adorn, Equip is a revolution against the beige melamine which characterizes much of disability design—a riot of color, energy and infinite variety which mirrors the lives of the disabled people I know, and which contrasts sharply with the medicalized, commercial products that most disabled people are forced to accept in their lives."[8]

introducing critical design

Within design, a technique has emerged that builds on the roles of contemporary art, literature, and filmmaking. Anthony Dunne and Fiona Raby are pioneers of critical design, which they define as "design that asks carefully crafted questions and makes us think," as opposed to "design that solves problems or finds answers."[9] Dunne is a professor of Design Interactions, an interdisciplinary program at the Royal College of Art. This indicates the significance of critical design within design culture and suggests that its influence will grow further.

utopia and dystopia

In the Energy Gallery at London's Science Museum, among numerous interactive exhibits that examine the future of energy production, Dunne & Raby created a simple, static triptych depicting a world employing new sources of bioenergy: electric energy derived from living matter, in this case not plants, but animals. At first glance the beautiful photography implies a utopian vision. On closer inspection, however, the scenes are more disturbing. A little girl leaves for school with her lunch box. The food is in one half of the container; the other half, labeled "poo," is for her to bring her excrement home as an energy source. In another scene, two children are surrounded by colorful mouse cages on the floor of their living room. Then you notice that one of the children is feeding a mouse into the television. Displayed alongside is a copy of a book titled *Animals for Energy: Avoiding Emotional Attachment to Animals Purchased for Use as Energy.*

The images reflect back to us some of the social implications of technical possibilities. They are neither an advertisement for nor a campaign against alternative energy sources. Brought to life like this, we can immerse ourselves in these possible futures as never before, except in fiction and film, and reflect on them.

Being beautifully designed in every visible detail, they deny us the excuse that this is just an *ugly* dystopian vision: we are required to reflect on objections other than aesthetic. Lest unconvincing detail get in the way, critical design is usually played *straight-faced* with products and media visualized in fine detail. It is then unclear whether to take it literally or not, and this ambiguity is deliberate. Since the questions may be difficult ones, critical design often relies on being uncomfortable in order to elicit a strong reaction and therefore engage an audience.

Not only is critical design distinct from the design of actual products; Dunne & Raby are careful to distance it from the kind of *concept design* typically undertaken within industry. Critical design "is related to haute couture, concept cars and visions of the future, but its purpose is not to present the dreams of industry, attract new business, anticipate new trends or test the market. Its purpose is to stimulate discussion and debate amongst designers, industry and the public."[10] The distinction with commercial design is not that the products may be unresolved or futuristic but that future resolved products are not even the eventual outcome. Freed from reconciling the commercial priorities of usability, desirability, and viability, critical design concerns itself with challenging existing values: social, cultural, technical, and economic. Design is used as a tool for exploring and challenging these values, rather than a means to respond to current consensus. However ambitious and imaginative so-called blue-sky concept designs are, it is surprising how ideologically conservative they usually are—how frequently they leave existing values and assumptions unchallenged. More often than not they imply that the future will be a fairly predictable evolution of the present, and in so doing, they market current businesses as well as perpetuate existing programs of research and development.

emotional prostheses

Other groups are also experimenting critically with the relationship between technology and the body. The word *prosthesis* gets used a lot in this context, and whether it refers to an artificial replacement for a part of the body or a broader idea of augmenting the body's abilities through technology, there is always some relevance to design and disability. In Chris Csikszentmihályi's Computing Culture group at the MIT Media Lab, researcher Kelly Dobson is inspired by "the advent of the cyborg."[11] She tells me that there are thousands of disabilities that she is inspired to design for, but in saying this she is not restricting herself to conventional notions of disability.

One of her projects is *Scream Body*, an external body organ for people who are unable to vent frustration or anger in public, so are condemned to carry this anger around unhealthily inside them.[12] A person wanting to scream but finding herself in a place where she feels inhibited, can instead yell into *Scream Body*, a bag she wears on her chest. The bag is well insulated, and so the scream isn't heard in the environment around her, although this means that it hasn't really been vented yet. Later, away from other people, she can open the bag and the captured scream is liberated noisily into the atmosphere. The anger is finally released. Concepts such as *Scream Body* are valuable contributions to any discussion of technology and the body because they challenge conventional boundaries. Exclusion is increasingly recognized as being broader than just sensory, motor, and cognitive; cultural issues are certainly part of the whole, and perhaps also emotional ones.

Scream Body by Kelly Dobson

critical design for disability?

The few concept design projects concerning more traditional disabilities tend to be uncritical in their optimism about the future role of technology, whether of *smart homes* of the future or omniscient domestic robots. Critical design addressing the same areas could provide a healthy balance and provoke much-needed discussion. Yet despite having been applied to issues as diverse as electromagnetic radiation, urban loneliness, and fortune-telling by designers such as Dunne & Raby, Noam Toran, and Crispin Jones, there is little evidence of critical design being applied to the issues around disability. Indeed, one can anticipate several objections to critical design for disability: wastefulness, insensitivity, or frivolity.

Wastefulness is a sensitive issue in itself, because a common frustration for disabled people and those developing products with them is how underinvested this area is when compared with mainstream consumer markets. An imperative to produce something immediately useful, given such pressing unmet needs, can make anything else seem unethical. Even user testing of early concept prototypes can be controversial, because users would like to be able to keep the prototypes and have them modified to their own individual needs.

The justification again comes from not confusing critical design with concept design but instead seeing them as complementary activities, with the role of critical design being to provide quite different insights and perspectives. And while these might ultimately inspire new paths for development, they might equally prove more disruptive, challenging the assumptions on which existing development is built. There is evidence of high levels of abandonment of assistive products that work, technically, but are rejected for other reasons. The assumption is often that this implies a lack of skill and confidence in using a device, but occupational therapist Clare Hocking has argued that abandonment also "relates to people's perception of themselves as disabled, and to broader issues of identity."[13] It therefore seems appropriate to invite challenges and a certain amount of disruption to our current assumptions.

uncomfortable ideas

Another objection is that critical design might be too uncomfortable and so appear insensitive. Although it represented a cutting edge of design meeting disability, RNID's HearWear project, already introduced in the chapters **fashion meets discretion** and **identity meets ability,** was largely a concept design project; the responses were in the main proposed as literal solutions. But given how irrational the stigma associated with wearing hearing aids is in many ways, yet how real, it is likely to take more than just optimistic design to change attitudes. The additional challenge of critical design might help.

Critical design is already being applied to the opportunities and contradictions afforded by biotechnology. Among students in the Design Interactions master's program at the Royal College of Art exploring the "social, cultural and ethical consequences of emerging technologies," there is a lot of interest in biotechnology and prostheses in the broadest sense.[14] Also at the Royal College of Art, Tobie Kerridge and Nikki Scott have explored jewelry made from laboratory-grown human bone tissue.[15] It could have been thought provoking to see some of this thinking applied to HearWear. This is controversial territory, sensitive in different ways for people who are Deaf with a capital D or deaf with a little d, to be explored with them rather than on their behalf. But at a time when technology affords the possibility of redesigning hearing itself, it does seem relevant to challenge our assumptions about the relationship between a hearing aid and its wearer. Several of the HearWear concepts that fitted onto or into the ear evoked jewelry, yet piercings and other jewelry often change the body as well as adorn it.

inappropriate humor

A third objection might be that critical design is too frivolous an approach for the seriousness and profundity of the issues around disability. There is certainly a dark humor behind critical design projects, and sometimes the humor is even more overt.

Social Mobiles was a collaboration between artist and designer Crispin Jones and IDEO. For IDEO, a design consultancy well-known for designing with users in mind, critical design allowed the user-centered, individual-centric priorities of the cell phone industry to be challenged, prioritizing the people around the user for a change. This allowed for a change in perspective from *my* phone to *their* phone. "We are interested in the frustration and anger caused by other people's mobile phones."[16]

In 2002, cell phones were becoming ubiquitous in Britain, and as a consequence everyone's experience of public spaces was beginning to be affected by inappropriate sounds from the phones and inconsiderate use by their owners. When the *Today* programme on BBC Radio 4 had a poll celebrating the centenary of the Patent Office, and listeners were asked to nominate their favorite and least favorite inventions, the telephone appeared in the top ten favorites, whereas the cell phone was among the ten least favorites, alongside land mines and nuclear weapons.

Social Mobiles are a series of five extreme phones that in different ways modified their users' behavior to make it less socially disruptive. These phones are quite ridiculous as first sight, but their audience can reflect on whether these interventions are any more ridiculous than the social disruption we all take for granted.

To set the tone, the first phone, *The Electric Shock Mobile*, delivers a painful voltage to its user, depending on how loud the person on the other end of the phone is speaking. In this way, the two parties are induced to whisper into their phones

The Electric Shock Mobile from *Social Mobiles* by IDEO and Crispin Jones

for fear of hurting the other, thereby causing less offense to those around them. It was proposed that people convicted of repeated offenses for cell phone misuse would have their own phones confiscated and be issued this phone instead.

Another phone, *The Musical Mobile*, turns the previously discreet act of dialing into a performance in itself, akin to playing a musical instrument in public. At this stage, the user can be made more self-conscious of the effect one is having on others—a timely litmus test as to whether it is appropriate to make a call in the first place. It is too late once we immerse ourselves in our conversation, when we may be genuinely oblivious to those around us.

The phones are deliberately large and old-fashioned, partly because they were working prototypes with existing phones and circuit boards built inside them, but also to make it clear that this was not a project about how phones *look* but how they *behave*. Each was photographed in the context of an everyday scenario, pulling back to take in people around the phone and its user. The scenes are clearly set in London, because the social inhibitions that prevent English people from just confronting each other over unacceptable behavior are not universal. But the project resonated with other cultures, especially Japan, with its rich tensions between embracing modern technology and respecting traditional social etiquette.

Social Mobiles was never intended to find a *solution* to antisocial cell phones but rather to provoke public discussion. In this respect it succeeded, with articles in the *Economist*, the *Independent* in the United Kingdom, *Wired* in the United States, *Axis* in Japan, and newspapers in a dozen countries as well as on radio and television worldwide.[17] It also seeded conversations with manufacturers and network operators about the relationship between technology, design, and social etiquette, and a change in perspective from the user to those affected by them.

Returning to disability, taking different perspectives could also be valuable. Disabled people's experiences are not just

The Musical Mobile from *Social Mobiles* by IDEO and Crispin Jones

directly affected by their disability but also by how it affects others, and by their own perceptions of this and the perceptions of others too. This implies considering the experiences of people around the user as well as that of the user themselves—perceptions as well as direct effects. Critical design could help to explore and provoke insights from new perspectives.

But should the approach taken on *Social Mobiles* ever be applied to an issue around disability? Showing an ambiguous or ridiculous response to an issue might seed serious discussions about what might not be so ridiculous. Does this come with the risk of ridiculing people with disabilities, though? Would the designers or a public audience be laughing with them or at them? One justification comes from the respect inherent in treating disability and accessibility with the same openness as other important design issues. Critical design is a lens best trained on profound yet underdiscussed issues. Design for disability deserves this attention.

"isn't it nice that they have their own website?"

Ultimately, the best defense of critical design is that more provocative attitudes are to be found among people with disabilities themselves. Disabled people routinely employ ambiguity and irony themselves to undermine attitudes toward their disabilities that they find unacceptable.

Damon Rose runs the BlindKiss website, an independent countercultural site for people with visual impairment.[18] Its antiestablishment nature is epitomized by a running joke of irreverently referring to the official RNIB as the RNLI (the acronym for the Royal National Lifeboat Institute).

The tone of BlindKiss mirrors, ridicules, but only slightly exaggerates existing attitudes to visually impaired people with the tagline "Isn't it nice that they have their own website?" introducing "the antidote to the usual worthy websites about blind people. If you're looking for traditional support or ideas on how to cope with this *terrible affliction*, then, um, this may not be the place for you. We're here to explode some of those media notions that being blind is some kind of living death, a mystical twilight state or a call to bravely climb mountains."[19]

supersafe products for blind people

And here on the BlindKiss site I find my best example of critical design applied to disability. "New supersafe products from RNIB" features parodies of well-meaning but patronizing aids to daily living intended to protect blind people from others and themselves. Among the blunted knives and forks and high-visibility clothing are these accessories that manage to parody visually impaired people's assumed sensory abilities and fashion sense:

> Trendy nose pegs. The world is a smelly place, and, as we all know, blind people are especially sensitive to smell. This nose peg can be clipped on to your nose when you are out and about to protect you from the general sweatiness of other people. For the more dress conscious among you, the nose peg comes in a variety of colours to match your outfit—including florescent yellow to match the [high-visibility belt] above. Price £4 for one, or £10 for bumper pack of three (colours randomly chosen).

Being a website written by visually impaired people for visually impaired people, the trendy nose pegs are described in text. Even in this context, designers collaborating to create arresting imagery might draw other people toward this story or encourage journalists to write about it for their readers.

exploiting critical design

Critical design need not be exploitative if applied to the issues around disability. Instead, disability groups could exploit critical design as a tool to provoke discussion about issues that may otherwise go undiscussed—in particular, the often unspoken assumptions inherent in current development and design for disability. Should hearing aids be invisible? Should prostheses mimic human flesh? Should it matter what equipment for visually impaired people looks like? Should the goal of assistive technology always be independence rather than interdependence?

feeling meets testing

Duncan Kerr, Mat Hunter, Jane Fulton-Suri, Marion Buchenau
The Wizard of Oz, Duane Bray, Roger Orpwood, Helen Petrie
Bill Gaver, Anthony Dunne, and Fiona Raby
Kodak camera and Spyfish underwater video, Health Buddy and Placebo
the Gloucester smart house and The Curious Home
Drift Table and Electro-draft Excluder

building Social Mobiles

testing

In medical engineering, prototypes are traditionally built to establish technical feasibility and allow for testing with users—an activity still often referred to as *clinical trials*. This term is inherited from a clinical culture, given that medical or biomedical engineering institutes are usually located within hospitals. In clinical research, treatments or solutions are proposed, and then need to be proven by testing and clinical trials. It is important that these trials are carried out in strictly controlled conditions in order to yield robust quantitative data from which the efficacy of a treatment can be proven. But this is certainly not the only role of testing in design in general. What other models of prototyping could also be beneficial within design for disability?

feeling

Within mainstream design, there is an increasing understanding that design is not confined to the creation of objects, if indeed it ever was. For example, in the area of interactive media, the distinction between a product, the content it delivers, and a service that it may be just a small part of is blurring. The role of design is broadening, and even a *user-centered* approach to design is no longer focused on issues of usability alone, but on the overall experience being created.

But whereas prototyping an object and assessing its fitness for purpose is relatively straightforward, prototyping an experience is more challenging. A range of techniques, collectively known as *experience prototyping*, has emerged to explore these new interactions with users. This chapter happens to be illustrated by pioneering work from IDEO and the Royal College of Art, but similar methods were also developed by other design groups in industry and academia, and are now employed worldwide.

tension

There are significant differences in the roles of these two types of prototyping and testing, and correspondingly in the methods employed. In each, the role of technology along with the context and spirit in which that technology is experienced can be quite different. And each will yield quite different material from the users in response.

A recent conference on assistive technology described its vision as "utility, usability and accessibility."[1] If these necessities are the extent of our vision, then traditional clinical testing could probably suffice. But more subjective and sensitive aspirations seem overdue: the engagement, experience, and emotion that a design elicits should be just as important, albeit in different ways in different areas of design for disability. Could experience prototyping be applied and evolved in the pursuit of these aspirations?

This chapter will introduce the practice of experience prototyping, with examples from consumer products and medical service design. Two contrasting case studies involving older people, with and without cognitive impairment, will be discussed. The chapter will end with longer-term, more open-ended testing conducted with the public in the context of two pioneering philosophies of design research, in which prototypes are not candidate solutions as much as they are tools and props in the hands and minds of their users.

experiencing the experience

When interaction designers Duncan Kerr and Mat Hunter were developing an early digital camera in the 1990s, they conceived a graphical user interface with animations that would respond to physical manipulation, a direct coupling of rotary switches, and a miniature screen. They searched for the most appropriate way to feel how intuitive and engaging this might be, and communicate this to their client, Kodak.[2]

Traditionally, multiple early prototypes would have been developed in parallel, associated with traditional design disciplines: ergonomists exploring handling and control layout through adjustable wooden rigs; industrial designers creating nonfunctioning appearance models to show form, color, and materials; the engineering team building and testing diverse rigs and breadboards to establish the technical feasibility of the components; and the recently recognized interaction designers creating a demo of the user interface on a computer screen, navigable via cursor and mouse. Only later on in a project would these prototypes converge in a fully working preproduction prototype, an investment of many person-hours, calendar months, and millions of dollars.

Their dilemma was that an on-screen demo did not communicate the interconnectedness of the physical and virtual interaction. Neither did an appearance model. They decided that they needed to get the interaction off the computer screen and into their hands. In Kerr's words, "The only way to experience an experience is to experience it."[3] And the best way to design the experience is to experience the design.

experience prototyping

So Kerr and Hunter built a different type of prototype, one in which the user's experience of the *interaction* was prioritized, at the expense of other qualities and criteria. This was a physical prototype with which you could *point* the camera to frame an image, *press* the shutter button to take a picture, *turn* a rotary switch to review your photos, and so on. But being built early and quickly, there were many compromises. It was much larger and cruder than the final design, or in essence a wooden box. A consumer video camera, a standard screen, and off-the-shelf knobs and switches were set into this box. Finally, an umbilical cord tethered the box to a computer running real-time image capture and animations.

H2Eye *Spyfish* STV submarine telepresence vehicle

The word *prototype* (in common with the word *design*) can be dangerously ambiguous, and if the role of any prototype is misunderstood, then people's expectations may be unrealistic and the prototype's value can be undermined. I have found it can be helpful to disentangle the many types of prototype, however crudely, being explicit about what a particular proto-type represents and what it does not. So an appearance model might be described as a *looks-like* prototype; a technical rig might be a *works-like* prototype; and an ergonomic rig might be a *feels-like* prototype. Then a weighted appearance model, in the right surface materials, might be a *looks-like-feels-like* prototype, and so on. The Kodak camera was a *behaves-like* prototype, but neither looked the same or worked with the same technology as the final product.

This *behaves-like* prototype also became the most valuable means of communicating the design intent within the client's organization, and in the end multiples were built for different stakeholders. Kerr now leads *behavior and interaction design* within Ive's industrial design group at Apple. Apple is notoriously secretive about its working methods, but clearly invests in crafting the experience.

Marion Buchenau and Jane Fulton-Suri coined a broader definition of *experience prototyping* to encompass activities that pri-oritize engaging people with an experience, even at the expense of fidelity to the design.[4] But they see experience prototyping less as a set of techniques than a "state of mind" directed to-ward allowing designers, users, and clients to "experience it themselves," rather than relying on demonstrations or proof of someone else's experience.[5]

feel, don't think

The *Spyfish* STV ("submarine telepresence vehicle") was a mini-ature remote-controlled submarine, a remotely operated ve-hicle (ROV). The dream of entrepreneur Nigel Jagger, *Spyfish* was the ROV reinvented as a leisure activity for yacht owners rather than a scientific tool for marine researchers. Jagger's company H2Eye developed a number of technical innovations to make this feasible; IDEO's role was to work with them to create a compelling user experience around this technology.

Professional ROV pilots require weeks of training before mastering the skill of controlling a complex vehicle in a moving sea. Could a leisure product ever be intuitive enough for members of the public to pick up? Yet was ease of use the ultimate goal, or might certain qualities and demands make for a more immersive experience?

As the first ideas developed, the interaction design team naturally wanted to try these out. But at the time, the submarine itself was a fragile prototype that could only be deployed in a test tank or, at best, a swimming pool—a finite environment where cursory exploration soon gave way to tests of maneuverability for its own sake. This is quite different from an unknown seascape, in which movement becomes a means to an end of discovery. How, then, to experience the experience?

The team found a submarine game for the Sony PlayStation, a virtual environment that represented many qualities of the final experience absent in the swimming pool: vast landscapes, shoals of fish, and a real sense of exploring the unknown. This might seem to contradict the Kodak project, in which a prototype in the hand was worth two on the screen, but it worked in this case, perhaps because video games are designed as experiences, unlike many computer simulations.

Nothing more sophisticated than flying leads, delicately soldered into a dismantled hand controller, allowed alternative controllers to be quickly built and tried out. A simple patch panel allowed control mappings—which switch controlled which action—to be changed around at will. The brief was a single-handed controller, leaving a hand free to steady oneself on a rocking boat. The first rig was nothing more than a PlayStation controller sawn in two, succeeded by pieces of plastic drainpipe with switches glued inside, and only later by carved wooden handles. Wilder ideas were also tried, such as seats built from skateboards, operated by leaning your body left and right, forward and back. After just a few weeks, two embryonic hand controllers had emerged that the whole team could try out.

The question each time was not so much about usability as whether the effort is outweighed by the enjoyment. Is it fun yet? Are you ready to let someone else have a go? This approach marked a turning point in the design process: where previously discussions had been conjectural and endless, now they were rooted in experience and decisive. Later, as soon as the submarine was more robust, these decisions could be confirmed and refined with the real thing.

behind the object; around the user

A design team might consider themselves to be creating an experience, but this doesn't mean that they are defining everything about the user's experience themselves. In the case of interactive products such as computers and phones, third-party content and communication with other people are experienced through the object; with cameras and submarines, the world around you or the sea below is experienced. The context or background contributes too; the environment, the weather or atmosphere, the social situation, and the user's mood all influence his or her overall experience.

So it becomes valuable to think not only of what to include in the prototype but also to consider carefully where and how to use it. An effort was made to use the *Spyfish* experience prototype in a relaxed environment, away from desks or workbenches, but using it on a moving boat, somewhere sunny, during a lazy holiday, could have contributed even more to the experience. With a project as inherently technological as this, it is too easy for the whole design process to be tied to the ongoing technical development, conducted in the laboratory or this state of mind. Experience prototyping can be a healthy antidote to this perspective.

This complexity of people's fuller experience could be seen as a problem, as extra dimensions of variability and subjectivity. User testing is more traditionally carried out in a *usability lab*, in which the variability of everyday contexts is eliminated to better establish the cause of a user's reaction and allow more direct comparisons between different trials. Experience prototyping is more likely to embrace subjectivity and idiosyncrasy.

behind the curtain; under the tablecloth

So far we have considered two fairly technological prototypes in which a personal computer masqueraded as a much simpler camera and a video console served as a submarine. But the prototyping technology really doesn't matter, as long as the experience is ultimately feasible with the final technology. A technological sledgehammer can be used to crack a nut, or a simpler technology can stand in for a more complex one.

At its most extreme, it can sometimes be quickest and quite acceptable to fake an interaction by having a member of the design team intervene. This is sometimes known as *Wizard of Oz* prototyping because of the scene in the film when the wizard, exposed as a fake, tells Dorothy to "pay no attention to that man behind the curtain." A suspension of disbelief may be agreed between users and designers, or the intervention may even go undetected. Despite their artifice, these *smoke-and-mirrors* experiments can be the least ambiguous of prototypes because their role is so clearly about the experience, not about the technology.

Interaction designer Duane Bray employed a mix of these two approaches, high-tech and low-tech, when designing the Health Buddy product. This is an Internet-connected appliance that asks patients a daily series of questions about how they are feeling. Automated checks and online experts remotely monitor the patients' answers as part of a service offered by the Health Hero Network. The promise is that people might continue to live independently in their own home with more reassurance that if their health does deteriorate, maybe in ways they are not aware of themselves, support will be at hand.

The user interface presented a particular challenge because the target market included older people. It was important to test older users' experience of the system. Bray and his team made a rough cardboard cutout of the device, with dummy cardboard buttons, and stuck this over a computer screen so that only a small window representing the text display on the device showed through. In testing, a person would sit in front of the model, read the text on the display, and answer questions by pressing one of the four cardboard buttons. Meanwhile, Bray sat with a keyboard balanced on his lap, out of sight under the table. Whenever the user pressed a fake button, Bray would press a corresponding key, and the simulation running on the computer would display the correct response to the user's action.[6]

Even this quick-and-dirty experience prototype was sufficient to reveal that many users were confused by conventions that most of us take for granted. Expressions such as *Enter* in the context of a text field and even sentences that were grammatically incomplete—even just missing a final period or full stop—could prove baffling to those older people who had never used a computer, a cell phone, or an automated teller machine before. A familiarity with these user interfaces, so often assumed by developers, could not be relied on. Avoiding unfamiliar conventions allowed a cognitively and culturally as well as visually and manually accessible service. The portable prototype was taken to users' own homes and used in an appropriate context. Here, the distractions of home as well as its familiarity and security affected the user's engagement with the online questionnaire. A rough but portable prototype was far more valuable than a refined prototype tethered to a laboratory.

when rough is inappropriate

BIME also has a long tradition of testing in disabled users' homes. Its core process of iterative user testing usually involves a series of prototypes, each of which advances the technical and user aspects of a design in tandem. It may start off with relatively crude so-called breadboard prototypes, and become more representative of the user's experience as the project progresses. This can therefore require that users try to see past the shortcomings of rough early mock-ups as part of the collaboration.

But BIME has found one area of its work where it has to make an exception. Exposing people with dementia to unresolved and unreliable prototypes can be disorienting and even upsetting to them. Within a clinical framework, this is automatically an ethical issue. So in this instance, BIME takes a different approach from its usual philosophy of directly involving end users throughout, first testing the ideas with personal carers on the users' behalf, which is "a judgment by proxy," admits BIME's director, Roger Orpwood.[7] Later on, end users will be exposed to an evolved and robust prototype, although admittedly at a point in the design process where changes can be less readily made, at an increased cost.

Direct testing with people with dementia is still necessary, however, because their reactions may be counterintuitive, even to their own carers. Orpwood describes an instance of this during the development of the Gloucester smart house, where researchers are employing assistive technology in an attempt to improve the quality of life of people with dementia and their carers.[8] Some people with dementia get confused about the time and get up in the middle of the night, as if it were morning. Sensors in a house could detect this easily enough, but the team wondered what kind of reminder could be triggered. The solution that eventually seemed to work best was to play a recorded message. It sounds like a recipe for confusion, and engineers and carers "felt that hearing a disembodied voice would freak users out. But it didn't."[9] The sound is made to come out of a radio, again potentially confusing since it is not a radio program, and yet "a radio seems to work, I believe because that is where the user expects a voice to come from," says Orpwood.[10] If these radio messages are recorded in the voice of a friend or family member, which again might have been confusing as to whether the person was on the radio or in the next room, this too is accepted and seems to have the advantage of being less habituating, of being less likely to become ignored over time. All of which illustrates how difficult it is to make judgments about simple behaviors without putting them to the test.

Perhaps experience prototyping could play a stronger role in this context. A prototype would need to deliver a refined experience, but if it didn't matter how this were technically achieved, less obvious techniques might allow earlier testing with people with dementia themselves, and at a point where ideas were still being explored and expanded. Helen Petrie at the University of York makes a careful distinction between *formative* and *summative* user testing: formative testing takes place early on, at a stage when radical disturbances can be welcomed as a step forward, not a step back.[11] But more usual is summative testing, in which a firm proposal is exposed to users, in the hope that they will accept it. Both have distinct complementary roles. The dilemma with experience prototyping is the effort required to create a representative enough experience. Too quick and dirty a prototype may demand too much *squinting* to see past its rough edges to be truly immersive. Too much time spent rounding off these edges runs the risk of a prototype with so much invested in its creation that it becomes a summative prototype by default. This is the value of experience prototypes, which can be made more convincingly, earlier on in the design process, than technical prototypes. Experience prototyping can fill the wide gap between early interviews and later clinical trials with full prototypes.

Drift Table, part of *The Curious Home* by Bill Gaver's research group

By the stage of formal trials, many decisions have had to be made already—decisions that earlier, more exploratory proto-typing could inform.

living with a prototype

Smart homes are a theme within assistive technology because of the issues around independent living, and so new roles for technology within the home are being pioneered. Meanwhile, designers are exploring the domestic environment in different ways—from diverse starting points, with different methods, and with differing motives.

The Interaction Research Studio at Goldsmiths College, University of London have exhibited *The Curious Home*.[12] Bill Gaver's team built a family of pieces of interactive furniture, which challenged the use of technology to support work, consumption, or entertainment. "Instead, technology can encourage more exploratory engagements with life, providing evocative resources with which to discover new perspectives on ourselves and the world around us."[13]

Part of this project, the *Drift Table*, is a coffee table with a small porthole window at its center, through which a small section of a satellite image of the British Isles is visible. There are strain gauges in the table legs, and leaning on one side or the other will gently drag the view in that direction. The experience suggests floating in a hot air balloon, looking down at the earth through the wrong end of a telescope. The *Drift Table* involves a formidable amount of technology, but this is seamlessly integrated into an unintimidating piece of furniture, which has been left with people in their own homes, to play with at their leisure, over a period of weeks rather than minutes. In the narratives that were returned with the furniture, one owner had been on elaborate journeys of hundreds of miles by stacking books at deliberate points on the edge of the table and leaving them there for hours on end. This kind of playful exploration of the purpose and experience of

detail of *Drift Table*

technology, often with no preconceived goal in mind, is the spirit of what Gaver refers to as *ludic design*, and reminds us that technology and design have roles beyond performing tasks or solving problems.

Returning to critical design, Dunne and Raby have also arranged for people to adopt their prototypes. Their *Placebo* project focused on perceptions of the invisible electromagnetic radiation that surrounds us: long-range signals from broadcast media and mobile communication networks along with more localized radiation from electronic products.[14] This radiation's very invisibility inhibits awareness, yet we are all likely to have tacit beliefs and feelings about its effects on our health and privacy. In order to engage the public in discussion, Dunne & Raby's team built a range of simple but enigmatic products. Some were technically sophisticated, and others less so, including the *Electro-draft Excluder*, a screen that people could supposedly hide behind to provide temporary relief from ambient background radiation.

These pieces of furniture were exhibited at the Victoria and Albert Museum in London, and visitors were invited to apply to adopt them—to take an exhibit home for a number of weeks, and record the way they used it and the way they grew to thinking about it. In the interviews that followed, the participants shared their experiences and perceptions. Often these reflections took the people themselves by surprise. Lauren Parker, who adopted the *Electro-draft Excluder*, for example, commented, "I hadn't expected that it would make me feel more insecure [about radiation] in my house, you just assume you get this protective thing and you'd feel protected. I didn't really think you could have something in your house that just made you more sensitive to things."[15]

In these roles, prototypes can act as tools around which new behaviors can emerge, or as props around which people can create their own narratives. More traditional clinical trials, focusing on usability and achieving tasks, would not elicit these

Electro-draft Excluder from the *Placebo* project by Dunne & Raby

responses. It would be challenging but appropriate to apply this kind of experience prototyping to design and disability. Issues of self-confidence, security, and just feeling comfortable with something can take time to emerge, and are influenced by the qualities and details of a design, not just its functionality. Adopting even a nonfunctioning prototype could allow a person to live with this new manifestation of her disability for a while and see how her feelings evolved with an increasing familiarity. It might allow her to conduct her own experiments, and observe the reactions of friends and strangers. This truly puts the individual at the heart of the process.

feeling the way forward

As with any other design, the acceptability of design for disability depends not just on its functionality and usability but also on how using it makes an individual feel. Experience prototyping can help make this tangible from the outset, and therefore as influential as more technical and clinical considerations. In even more radical roles, prototypes can become tools and props, allowing behaviors to emerge and eliciting reflection.

If experience prototyping is to find a complementary role alongside clinical trials in design for disability, it is important that their differences be acknowledged. If experience prototyping is judged by the standards of traditional clinical trials, it could be undervalued for its perceived lack of rigor. But if the differences between the approaches are embraced, the investment in these new methods could advance our ability to design within people's broader experience of their disability and lives.

expression meets information

David Crystal, Alan Newell, Annalu Waller
Art Honeyman, Erik Blankinship, Stephen Hawking, Laurie Anderson
Ben Rubin, Mark Hansen, Duncan Kerr, Heather Martin, Violeta Vojvodic
Richard Ellenson, Erik Spiekermann, Somiya Shabban
Johanna Van Daalen, and Deirdre Figueiredo
nine ways to say "yes" and seventeen ways to say "really"
The Speaking Mobile and Listening Post, recording poems and communicating kisses
the Dictionary of Primal Behaviour and Tango!

detail of *The Speaking Mobile*

information

One of the most challenging applications of assistive technology is for communication by people with speech and language impairments. This field is also known as Augmentative and Alternative Communication (AAC), and covers a wide range of media including voice output communication aids. Decade by decade, synthetic speech technology is improved to sound less robotic and more human, and to automatically place stresses and intonation so that sentences are not misunderstood and information is successfully communicated.

There is a tendency to see this ongoing technical development as the means to better communication. Just as prosthetics is dominated by a goal of *realistic* forms, and hearing technology by *invisible* hearing aids, so communication technology tends to be seen as a quest for so-called natural speech. The ideal would seem to be a *transparent* medium, which doesn't get in the way of the message or obscure its meaning. But is the elimination of misunderstanding and ambiguity always the highest goal for a communication aid?

expression

Of course, human communication is as much about social interaction as it is about conveying information. The quantity of information or the accuracy with which it is transmitted is often less significant than its qualities; *what* is said is often less important than *how* it is said.

To a designer, this mix of the quantitative and qualitative sounds at once familiar, challenging, and inspiring. I believe that designers could make a valuable contribution to AAC. As in so many areas of design, designers could help people to better express themselves, perhaps in ways just not supported at the moment.

tensions

Clearly there are tensions arising from the nature of communication itself, in reconciling the relative importance of information and expression. Whether *unambiguous* communication is more crucial than *engaging* communication depends on the social context and the individual's priorities.

There are also the familiar disciplinary tensions. AAC is already rich, interdisciplinary territory involving speech therapists, clinicians, carers, people with speech and language impairments themselves, phoneticians, linguists, speech technologists, computer scientists, and human-computer interaction specialists. Yet once again, there is little recognition that designers, not even interaction designers, have a role to play at all. Few are involved, which is one reason that the author is conducting design research in this area.

But this area would also provoke tensions within design culture itself. How does the nature of design change when the user's self-expression is more important than the designer's own, and when the user is not just expressing himself indirectly through his choice of design but directly through its use? What is then the role of the designer? Again, answers from design for disability could enrich design as a whole.

This chapter will consider all three of these tensions, starting with the way that not just meaning but also identity are conveyed through tone of voice. It expands to explore expression through poems, kisses, boos, and whispers. A case study involving some of the world's most experienced design firms is complemented by a collaboration between an individual designer and a young person with complex communication needs who together created a refreshingly simple and provocative piece—an exemplar of what can happen when design meets AAC.

nine ways to say "yes"

"It ain't what you say, it's the way that you say it," as the song goes. The meaning of the simplest utterances depends as much on tone of voice as the choice of words. The word *yes* can be delivered as a positive, affirmative response to a question, but said differently, it can express detachment, sarcasm, disbelief, or tentativeness instead, undermining the questioner rather than agreeing with or reassuring them. Linguist David Crystal has illustrated this with intonation diagrams of nine different ways of responding "yes" in English to the same question, but he says that "no-one has yet described all of the nuances of meaning that can be conveyed by the intonation system."[1] Nine ways is nowhere near the richness of expression that most speakers employ.

In contrast, users of current communication aids have little or no control over intonation. Most systems are based on text-to-speech technology. Text is typed in, or if the person cannot use a keyboard, letters, words, or pictures might be selected from a menu. A computer then transcribes this text into a sequence of phonemes based on a pronunciation dictionary, from which synthesized speech is generated. The more sophisticated systems use linguistic algorithms to determine where stresses should be placed and what intonation might make the sentence sound most *natural*, but the user cannot influence this outcome. If only typing or selecting text, the user's last resort is punctuation, and some communication aids change the inflection of a sentence if it ends with an exclamation mark or a question mark, giving three choices in all: so-called neutral, exclaiming, and questioning. But there is never control of what *quality* of questioning, whether fascinated, outraged, or skeptical, and so on. Phonetician John Holmes has noted that "spoken and written language are different in many ways, and speech has the ability to capture subtle shades of meaning that are quite difficult to express in text, where one's only options are in choice of words and punctuation."[2]

... It is advantageous to show the stress on the intonation. This is conveniently done by showing stressed syllables ... dots. If a syllable with a rising or falling intonation is ... this may be shown by placing a large dot on the appro-... part of the curve (generally at the beginning); so when ... has no dot attached to it, it is to be understood that the ... is unstressed.[3]

1016. Intonation is most important for indicating shades of meaning. Compare the following:

(meaning 'That is so')

jes.
Yes.

jes.
Yes.

(meaning 'yes, I understand that; please conti... This form is very frequently used when sp... on the telephone. The same intonation w... used in answering a question if a further... were expected; for instance a shopman... it in answering the question 'Do you keep...

(meaning 'Of course it is so')

jes.
Yes.

(meaning 'Is it really so?')

jes?
Yes?

(ordinary ...iry'

jes.
Yes.

'wot
Wha...

shades of meaning of "yes" from the fifth edition of *An Outline of English Phonetics* by Daniel Jones, published in 1936 by W. H. Heffer

So improving the expressiveness of communication aids may demand thinking about interacting with synthesized speech in a totally different way, not just advancing the underlying technology. Professor Alan Newell has been pioneering AAC research at the University of Dundee for twenty-five years and considers that the field has settled into rather conservative ways of approaching communication devices. As early as 1991, he was advocating a "paradigm shift" in thinking about AAC—a shift that has yet to take place.[3] Interaction designers could make a valuable contribution, complementing the human-computer interface specialists already in the field by bringing a design culture, design sensibilities, and design skills to our interactions with technology and communication with each other. Designing any communication aid is about designing interactions.[4]

playing with speech

One example of a radical new interaction with synthesized speech can be found in the *Social Mobiles* project, the extreme telephones that reduced antisocial behavior. The second phone in the series, *The Speaking Mobile*, didn't deter people from using their phone, but allowed them to speak with their hands, in circumstances where it would be inconsiderate to talk out loud. This inhibition could almost be viewed as a socially contextual speech impairment.

If text-to-speech offers a full vocabulary yet little or no control of intonation, *The Speaking Mobile* is all intonation, at the expense of vocabulary. In fact the user can say only "yeah" or "no," but can intone these any way they want to by manipulating their timing and pitch with a joystick. With practice, it is possible to produce all of the variants described by Crystal and more.

Can anything be learned from this extreme approach that might have relevance to communication aids?[5] In accordance with the principle of experience prototyping, a fully working

The Speaking Mobile in the hands of model maker Anton Schubert

phone was built that could be used on telephone calls. The experience of using it was that it was surprisingly effective in conversation. "Yes" and "no" are not restricted to answering straight questions. Interjecting more ambivalent "yes [sort of . . .]" or "no [not quite . . .]" responses can be used to skillfully steer a conversation toward a desired outcome. Also, people evolved a technique of curtailed "ye-yeahs" and "uh-huhs" to reassure the other person that they were still listening. On the telephone, when facial expressions cannot be seen, these interjections take the place of subconscious nodding, supporting and sustaining the conversation.

Amar Latif is a filmmaker, founder of the Traveleyes travel company, star of BBC's *Beyond Boundaries*, and a qualified, practicing accountant.[6] Latif defined what he found to be the worst thing about being blind. It was not, he said, as people might suspect, the inability to drive a car or watch a film. For him, it was the inability to read people's facial expressions when he was talking to them. Not to know if they were hanging on his every word, or whether they had lost interest and were already looking around the room for someone more interesting to talk to, although this is unlikely given Latif's warm but dry Glaswegian humor. Here is a resonance of needs between people on the telephone and visually impaired people.

With its emphasis on written language, text-to-speech tends to overlook these *paralinguistic* uses of speech in communication, and as a result so do most AAC devices. The author is leading design research at the University of Dundee that will adopt more radical approaches to synthetic speech, treating speech as sound as much as text, borrowing mental models from fields as diverse as sociolinguistics and stage directions, percussive instruments and psychology, and inspired as much by the earliest mechanical speech synthesizers as by computer technology.[7]

manipulation of intonation with *The Speaking Mobile*

seventeen ways to say "really"

Going beyond Crystal's nine ways of saying "yes," the historian Paul Johnson has been quoted as saying, "No man is truly English if he cannot say '*Really*' seventeen different ways." This statement may be ironic, but it expresses a broader role of subtle intonation: speech communicates not only the meaning of an individual sentence but also so much more about the identity and character of the speaker.

And the converse can be true. Annalu Waller, another researcher into AAC at Dundee University, is passionate about the way in which we all make judgments about a stranger's intelligence based on his or her first utterances. Waller has cerebral palsy herself and, even though her dysarthric speech is intelligible, has resorted to carrying academic books gratuitously under her arm when on a plane so that she'll be taken more seriously "as a person" by the cabin crew.[8] Her colleague Norman Alm worries that communication aids with a limited range of intonation can imply a corresponding limit to the emotional range and therefore the intelligence of their users.[9] If intonation cannot yet be controlled by the user of a communication aid, perhaps even a randomized variation of intonation might help its user to be taken more seriously. For Waller and Alm, this is not a ridiculous idea.

prose into poetry

For some people, language plays an even more central role in their identity. Art Honeyman is a poet who also happens to have cerebral palsy. He likes to leave his poems as messages—as gifts—on his friends' telephone answering machines, but was never happy with the monotonic delivery of his existing communication aid. Erik Blankinship, a researcher at the MIT Media Lab, worked with Honeyman to create Poemshop.[10] In the way that Adobe Photoshop allows the manipulation of photographs, so Poemshop allowed Honeyman to manipulate the sound of his synthesized poems. This trial interface was challenging to create and use, but it allowed Honeyman to hear and refine his delivery endlessly until he was happy with it, in a way an actor might rehearse a line, although all speech contains an element of performance. The role of intonation here is profound: to elevate prose into poetry and affirm Honeyman's identity as a poet.

finding your voice

Professor Stephen Hawking is the most famous user of a communication aid, although his situation is unusual among AAC users since he is more immune than most from the negative first impressions that this technology can attract. As a leading theoretical physicist, no one is likely to infer that Hawking is cognitively impaired just because of the way he is able to converse, although he has said that "one's voice is very important. If you have a slurred voice, people are likely to treat you as mentally deficient: does he take sugar?"[11] It has been reported that Hawking prefers not to ask too many questions, due to the awkwardness of their intonation. Such an inhibition could have a profound influence on any person's interaction with others.

Despite this, Hawking has declined an updated synthetic voice with so-called realistic speech, saying that the robotic-sounding speech is now "his voice." "The only trouble is that it gives me an American accent," explains Hawking, but do people ascribe that accent to him or to the U.S. technology?[12] It has become part of his public identity. He has even described it as his trademark. In his case, his fame and early adoption of speech technology gave him ownership of his new voice, whereas I have heard another AAC user describe an AAC event sounding like a room full of Stephen Hawkings.

speech as a design medium

The obvious artificiality of Hawking's speech may have actually helped avoid questions of whether his voice suits him or not. But as the technology progresses, what qualities will determine the acceptance of a synthesized voice by its user and the people they talk to? Just as some amputees can feel uncomfortable with a cosmetic prosthesis out of proportion with the rest of their body and so "not their hand," but also one that is too eerily realistic, even macabre, perhaps as the naturalness of text-to-speech improves, there may be interest in creating synthetic voices that are sensitive yet acknowledge their own artificiality.

Text-to-speech still tends to be treated far more as a technology than a designed medium, as if the quest for so-called natural speech obviates design decisions about the nature of its artificiality. Performance artist Laurie Anderson has said, "Technology today is the campfire around which we tell our stories."[13] Technology can be a vehicle for communication, yet it also colors it. It is never entirely transparent, and its qualities—its warmth, its brightness—can enrich or complicate our experience. At the moment, and perhaps for the foreseeable future, synthetic speech can be easily distinguished from human speech, and thus communication with an AAC device is never the same as communication without. Crafting the qualities of synthetic speech, working within the limits of the technology as it evolves, could in turn stimulate new directions for this technical development. Artists and designers have started to explore the medium of synthesized speech.

Listening Post is an art installation of hundreds of text displays and dozens of voices—voices that are overtly synthetic, yet absolutely beautiful.[14] Sound designer Ben Rubin and researcher Mark Hansen sample messages on the Web and translate them into synthesized speech. The many synthetic voices are each monotonic, but their pitches are tuned to notes on a scale and an ambient drone creates a soundscape reminiscent of a Gregorian chant. The strange thing is that although the voices are monotonic, they sound convincingly human because a context has been created in which they appear to be monotonic on

Listening Post by Ben Rubin and Mark Hansen

purpose, chanting rather than speaking. They sound sensitive and intelligent—positive qualities in communication aids.

The development of speech technology could be inspired by exploratory work like this, rather than always aiming for a model of natural speech. In the near future at least, it will not be possible to produce synthetic speech that sounds totally natural, so how should it sound instead? By analogy, when new fonts have been designed for showing text on low-resolution displays, they are not just pixelated samples of traditional printed typefaces but new typographic designs, designed pixel by pixel. Synthesized speech is also a design medium, but its qualities are still impoverished and the new design languages it could support are underexplored.

say it with a kiss

In their *Kiss Communicator*, Duncan Kerr and Heather Martin, who went on to Apple and the Copenhagen Institute of Interaction Design, respectively, explored a language beyond words and speech.[15] Alongside mobile communications based on voice and text, pictures and video, Kerr and Martin were interested in simpler, more abstract, but equally loaded media. Lovers would buy a boxed pair of *Kiss Communicators*, each dedicated to the other. When one lover blows into one of the communicators, a pattern of lights plays over its surface and is sent to the other device, wherever it is in the world. When their partner notices her device glowing gently, she can release this message and see the original pattern of lights created by the kiss played out on her own communicator. Once. Only once. No storing; no archiving. A kiss is ephemeral.

An experience prototype took the idea beyond words and started to explore the experience. What does it feel like to blow into an inanimate product? Does this feeling change if the product responds? Can you represent something as human as a kiss in the behavior of lights? Can light diffusing through plastic feel precious in the hand? To answer these questions,

eek /iːk/

an expression of sudden fear and surprise

hur.rah /hʊˈrɑː/

shouted when you are very glad about something

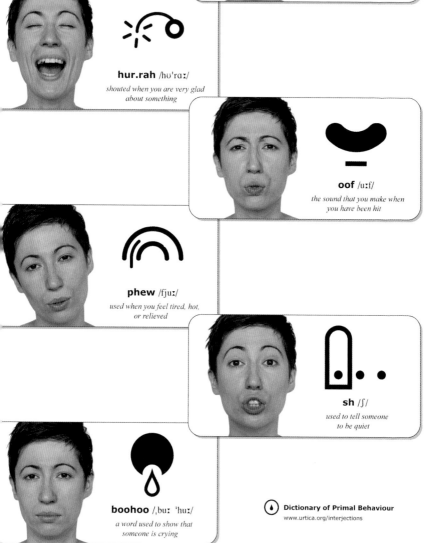

oof /uːf/

the sound that you make when you have been hit

phew /fjuː/

used when you feel tired, hot, or relieved

sh /ʃ/

used to tell someone to be quiet

boohoo /ˌbuː ˈhuː/

a word used to show that someone is crying

Dictionary of Primal Behaviour
www.urtica.org/interjections

interjections from Urtica's *Dictionary of Primal Behaviour* you need to experience the experience. The richness of communication does not depend on technical bandwidth; it is as much qualitative as quantitative, often as much about what the parties bring in their own minds as how much is transmitted over the network. How much data is required to define a kiss? How much information does it contain? What can be expressed?

Self-expression involves gestures and rituals as well as words and sounds, and is relevant to design for disability beyond dedicated communication aids. For example, any hand, even a prosthetic one, is not just a tool to hold things in but also an instrument of communication and expression. Some amputees have mentioned their embarrassment when giving directions in the street or waving at a friend using a clenched grip rather than a pointing finger or an open palm. Yet textbooks on prosthetic hands often restrict themselves to different types of prehension, the grasping or holding of objects. If only to introduce a fresh perspective, it would be provocative to strike a different balance between these roles, prioritizing expressive gestures for a change.

the aesthetic pleasure of communication

The art and media research group Urtica in Serbia has bridged verbal and nonverbal communication.[16] Violeta Vojvodic and Eduard Balaz are fascinated by what they term *common linguistic knowledge*: utterances common across many languages that represent strong feelings such as shock, pain, or pleasure. These include "aha," "boo," "eek," "hurrah," "oh," "oops," "ow," "wow," and "yuck." Urtica's *Dictionary of Primal Behaviour* represents thirty-eight interjections both phonetically and graphically, as sound recordings, photographs, and videos of facial expressions as well as graphic icons abstracted from these. The group is interested in the redundancy of this technique, and its potential role to accommodate disability as well as cultural and linguistic differences between speaker and listener.

Richard and Thomas Ellenson with Tango!

But Urtica is also intrigued by ambiguity and the room left for interpretation. It cites French information theoretician Abraham Moles's theory that aesthetic pleasure is determined by the balance of the originality of the message and the ability of the recipient to understand it.[17] Clearly intonation plays a role on both sides of this equation: it helps decipher meaning, but just as important, it affords more originality of expression. At the moment, it seems that AAC is more concerned with understanding than expression.

The *Dictionary of Primal Behaviour* is described as an art project, and not only is aesthetic pleasure a theme of the research, it is also manifest in its presentation. If this level of design were routinely brought to AAC, devices would be more satisfying to use, but also send out more positive signals about their users to others. Too often communication aids designed for adults look as though they are intended either for young children or computer programmers, and perhaps even designed by young children or computer programmers. In our culture we take for granted a visual sophistication in most things, from newspapers and book covers, to websites and packaging. How much more appropriate to find this in something as profound as a communication aid?

Tango!

Richard Ellenson is an advertising executive whose son, Thomas, has cerebral palsy. When Ellenson founded the company Blink Twice to create a product to help young children communicate, he did not attempt to design everything himself or even build a company that would design everything itself.[18] He approached it as he might have any major campaign: by seeking out a diverse cast of world-class specialists to each bring what they did best to the project. So he engaged not only the speech language professionals Pati King-DeBaun, Patrick Brune, and Beth Dinneen but also companies with no prior involvement in AAC: product design groups Smart

Somiya wearing the badge she designed with Johanna Van Daalen

Design and frog design, which brought the same sensibilities as they would to a product for able-bodied kids, while electronics manufacturing company Flextronics brought consumer-market technology and build quality. Ellenson even involved the kids' television network Nickelodeon to develop cartoon characters and voices for the interface, whereas the graphical user interfaces on most AAC devices have never even involved a graphic designer. "The sensibility that has infiltrated the toothbrush section of Target has not yet reached assistive technology and there is no world where first impressions are more important," says Ellenson.[19] Whatever our opinions of the excesses of toothbrush marketing, this is an incontrovertible yet chilling observation.

Tango!, the resulting product, has been compared to an overgrown Sony PSP (PlayStation Portable)—an appropriate and positive association given its target market and peer group. This attention to aesthetics is not just applied to the surface but from the inside out as well, from the fundamentals of the user interface itself. Even the choice of voice qualities is tuned to a child's need to express themselves in particular ways, between speaking, yelling, whispering, and whining. Tango! has set a new standard not just in AAC or assistive technology but also in design for disability in general.

you cannot not communicate

"You cannot not communicate" is a much-repeated statement attributed to Erik Spiekermann, founder of the graphic design group MetaDesign.[20] Whether or not graphics are consciously designed, they will inevitably express strong messages to different people, positive or negative. There is no such thing as a culturally *neutral* design language, and this applies equally to other modes of communication: a lack of intonation speaks volumes.

Communication aids are not a neutral technology or transparent medium. Alongside the messages they transmit, they

when Somiya uses her badge

inevitably send out other signals themselves. Their physical design, interactions, voice qualities, and intonation or lack of it all communicate something too. How important for these signals to have been considered as part of the design process and for the person using the device to be supported by these layers of communication, not undermined by them.

Somiya has the last word

Design for communication can be both simple and profound.

In order to communicate with other people, Somiya Shabban uses a dialogue book, in which she points to words or images. This is versatile, but it can be laborious. When Somiya was still at school, Johanna Van Daalen from the design group Electricwig worked with her to help her to express herself more fully. In particular, Somiya wanted the freedom to express frustration more spontaneously, so together they designed a badge that she could activate using a switch next to her head, whenever she wanted to.

When she does this, the badge lights up with the words "Somiya says SOD OFF."

This message is wonderfully direct and disarming, and yet the badge expresses so much more besides this information. It also communicates that she is the kind of person who will use this language; that she is the kind of person to whom this is important enough to dedicate a button to; and that she doesn't mind who knows this. Perhaps it seems inefficient to produce such a limited communication device, and one that can only be used for one sentence. But this is to ignore its other role: the short-term utterance is also a long-term badge—a label of Somiya's own devising, to express her individuality and identity, rather than any stereotype associated with her impairment.

This small project was part of an initiative called Designing for Access run by Craftspace.[21] For its director, Deirdre Figueiredo, involving individual designers and disabled individuals is about setting up a creative partnership. The design is done together: not by the designer for the individual, but neither by the individual using the designer just as a facilitator. It emerges from a dialogue and a relationship. In the area of personal communication especially, there is the challenge of how design itself changes if its goal is to support self-expression. How does the designer learn to let go and subsequently share authorship with the user? For Figueiredo, there is also an agenda that faces back toward the design community, because "disability contributes to the wider development of crafts and design practices."[22]

So what was the role of the designer in this particular exercise in self-expression? To realize the detailed visual design, certainly. The colors and typographic simplicity are in tune with the directness of the message, yet its visual innocence is playfully at odds with the wording. This is a more effective badge for being nicely designed, but design has played its part in the very conception of this piece. It manages to be both restrained and provocative. These are design sensibilities at work.

aesthetics in the broadest sense

It is one thing to design a chair for someone and quite another to help them find their voice. Any communication aid plays an even more profound role in the life of its owner than the wheelchairs and hearing aids previously discussed: it not only influences her identity, but how she converses with others, and this comes closer to her very personality. In the case of communication aids, the role of design is even more marginalized; surely these are linguistic prostheses after all, and not cosmetic products?

Aesthetic qualities are not usually considered in design for disability, and when they are it is often as an afterthought, a final cosmetic treatment of an already resolved and acceptable design. But it is impossible to disentangle our senses from our overall experience of a design, the visible from our social sensitivities, the tactile from our emotional response. Our interaction with any product is a complex web of sensory and contextual interactions, which is why products with the same functionality can succeed or fail for other reasons entirely. In design for disability, this may be not just an issue of market share but also of outright rejection of an assistive technology.

In AAC, aesthetics is not limited to the visual and tactile but encompasses the audible and other time-based qualities too. It includes the resistance and yielding of a button, the responsiveness of an auditory control, and the choreography of an animation. The consideration of aesthetics should extend from the physical design to the interaction design. Or rather, it should expand from the heart of the product outward—from the expressiveness afforded by the interaction to the voice quality and the industrial design, the physical manifestations of these inner qualities. Each sends out its own messages.

Interaction designers and industrial designers, graphic designers and sound designers, even fashion designers and furniture designers, could contribute so much to AAC and design for disability in general. There is a place here for many of the values of art school design: exploring and feeling, simplicity and provocation, identity and expression.

meetings with designers

Sandy Marshall, Tomoko Azumi, Philippe Starck, Jasper Morrison
Michael Marriott, Hussein Chalayan, Martin Bone, Jonathan Ive
Paul Smith, Graham Cutler, Tony Gross, Huw Morgan
Andy Stevens, Tord Boontje, Crispin Jones, Durrell Bishop
Julius Popp, Andrew Cook, Anthony Dunne, Fiona Raby
Stefan Sagmeister, Adam Thorpe, and Joe Hunter

uplifting stools and wry bottom wipers, social and cultural chairs and political capes
material legs and conceptual arms, accurate wristwatches for exacting people
visible and decorative braille, dairy-free accessibility signage
refined and extravagant hearing aids, interactive and ephemeral text displays
expressive communication aids and provocative memory aids

when Vexed meets wheelchair capes

diverse meetings

Disabled people do not all share a single experience, even of the same impairment; likewise, designers in the same discipline do not follow a single approach or hold the same values. Exciting new directions will arise from individual designers working with disabled individuals on particular briefs. This will produce different responses each time, complementary and even contradictory directions, but this richness is needed. This section offers just a glimpse of future possibilities, juxtaposing leading designers with projects to which they could be well suited.

> Tomoko Azumi meets step stools
> if Philippe Starck met bottom wipers
> if Jasper Morrison met wheelchairs
> Michael Marriott meets wheelchairs
> if Hussein Chalayan met robot arms
> Martin Bone meets prosthetic legs
> if Jonathan Ive met hearing aids
> if Paul Smith met hearing aids
> if Cutler and Gross met hearing aids
> Graphic Thought Facility meets braille
> if Tord Boontje met braille
> Crispin Jones meets watches for visually impaired people
> if Durrell Bishop met communication aids
> if Julius Popp met communication aids
> Andrew Cook meets communication aids
> if Dunne & Raby met memory aids
> if Stefan Sagmeister met accessibility signage
> Vexed meets wheelchair capes

Some (the "ifs") are two pages, and others are fuller interviews—discourses illustrating the way that a designer might approach a particular brief. These are first trains of thought, nothing more, but I hope that such meetings might inspire substantive projects in the future.

nested tables designed by Tomoko Azumi and Shin Azumi for Japanese furniture manufacturer nextmaruni

Tomoko Azumi meets step stools

Sandy Marshall, photographed for an interview in the *Guardian* newspaper

step stools

Sandy Marshall is four feet, two inches tall, the result of a restricted growth condition called achondroplasia. "The world is not made for someone like me. You need imagination to get over the hurdles," she says, describing visiting friends and not being able to reach the doorbell.[1] On lifts or elevators, she sometimes has to ride up as far as the highest button she can reach and then walk the remaining flights of stairs.

People with restricted growth often have their own homes made accessible for them, with light switches, door handles, and cupboards that they can comfortably reach, but outside in a world designed for people of normal stature, things can frequently be inaccessible.

So when Roger Orpwood and Jill Jepsom at BIME conducted a survey of unmet needs among people with restricted growth, one of the highest priorities was a step stool: something that could be carried around anywhere its owner went, and occasionally used to stand on to increase their effective stature.

At first sight, this is a classic mechanical engineering and ergonomics design brief: a step stool must be strong and stable when deployed because some people with restricted growth, despite their height, may not be of such restricted weight. Yet it also should be lightweight to be carried easily, and probably needs to fold in some way so that it is not too bulky when not in use, implying some kind of mechanism. This is a brief in which, as is frequently the case with products for people with disabilities, the technical issues can all too easily dominate.

But this is not just an engineering challenge: when its owner is carrying it around, the step stool will be noticed by people they meet and will form part of their initial impression, as would a briefcase, a handbag, or an item of clothing. Orpwood says that beyond the obviousness of their disability, people with restricted growth are sensitive to the things around them and do not want to be stigmatized by assistive

Table = Chest by Tomoko Azumi, her degree showpiece at the Royal College of Art

devices. This is especially true of a product like a step stool that would be carried around and used in public.

Michael Shamash, like Sandy Marshall, has restricted growth and works for the Restricted Growth Association. He is passionate about design, and when faced with the same problem found himself in a fashionable London furniture store buying "an expensive and designerly" set of steps, which he describes as being attractive but not ideal for the purpose, because they were not designed with restricted growth in mind.[2]

This is not surprising, since the design brief for a step stool is rather different from that for a set of occasional domestic steps. For one thing, a step stool will need to be carried around a lot more, rather than left propped against a wall. More important, it will be used in public, so its appearance when folded, how it unfolds, and how its owner looks standing on it will inevitably become part of that person's projected image and identity. What different ideas might result if a step stool were approached from these more social and emotional perspectives?

Tomoko Azumi

When considering this change in perspective, the furniture and product designer Tomoko Azumi springs to mind. Her background was in environmental design, but she moved away from architecture toward furniture, preferring to work with "things that are in human scale, things that you can touch."[3]

Azumi then studied furniture design at the Royal College of Art, where her degree project, *Table = Chest*, was a three-drawer chest that transformed into a low table. *Table = Chest* wears its ingenuity so lightly: as either a chest or a table, it is quietly and beautifully resolved. In other hands, such a brief could have become so much more of a technical tour de force, an exercise in mechanism design. The forms of the table and chest are each inspired by their transformation, but

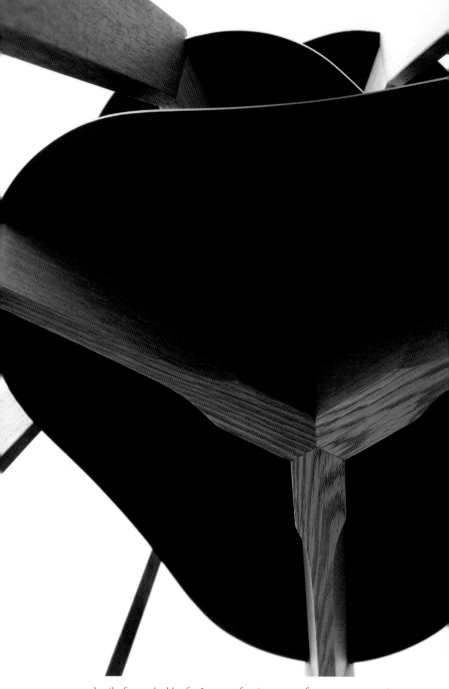

detail of nested tables for Japanese furniture manufacturer nextmaruni not dominated by it. Yet there is an understated delight in the unexpected transformation.

This emphasis on transformation and interactivity has remained a theme in Azumi's work. One of her favorite pieces of her own work is the Overture screen, manufactured by Lapalma, that rolls up into a tube for transportation. With her former design partner Shin Azumi, Tomoko Azumi created furniture for Isokon, crockery for Muji, and housewares for Authentics.

More recently, her own studio's work has included nested tables for the Japanese manufacturer Maruni.[4] Her work is characterized by its simplicity, but Azumi denies that it is minimalist; there is always a warmth, and often humor, more or less overt. It's tempting to say that the pieces have a *personality*. Her diverse work has been described in terms such as "minimalist yet sensual pieces that invite interaction."[5]

Her studio is evidence of her particular working technique. There are dozens of miniature models of concepts for furniture. Through these models, the ideas and details are explored and resolved in three dimensions. She may sketch her very first ideas, but moves to models and prototypes early on. When redesigning the classic Donkey bookcase for Isokon, Azumi presented thirty or more maquettes to unfold the thought process in front of the client, by way of a performance.[6]

When I visit her studio one day, a full-size production prototype of a coat stand is being discussed. The wooden pieces interlock in an ingenious but simple way, with the details of the joints clearly on display and part of the visual design. But there is a problem with the steam-bent wood opening up at these joints. On the prototype, these are being wrapped with string to hold them together, and Azumi is going over alternatives with the manufacturer and her design team. The devil is always in the detail.

meeting

As with many of the designers I have approached, Azumi was at pains to emphasize how underqualified she was, and how little she knew about disability and medical engineering. Yet our early conversation touched on some experiences that Azumi herself had when she first arrived in London, finding herself shorter relative to the British population than in her native Tokyo. She'd used bathrooms with mirrors that were mounted too high on the wall for her to be able to see herself, and cupboards that were too high to reach. Not to imply that this would qualify Azumi to design a step stool without the direct participation of people with restricted growth, but this source of empathy inspires her to design sympathetically and appropriately for them.

In an inspiring and meandering conversation, we found ourselves talking about some sort of analogy with musicians carrying their instruments in cases—the image of a musician struggling to carry a large instrument on to public transport, on a bus or a train. A 'cello case is certainly conspicuous and functionally inconvenient, yet somehow never stigmatizing. This human-made object seems a natural extension of its owner's character, and while much of this intimacy comes from the activity of playing music and the cultural value of this, nevertheless Azumi sees inspiration to be gained from it.

With this vision of musical instrument cases in mind, Azumi photographed young people walking around the city with their backpacks, noticing that these bags weren't necessarily small, but their soft materials and rounded forms lent them a friendly appearance. She became intrigued by a step stool that might not fold up at all, making it simpler but larger to carry around. Although a larger object may be more conspicuous, perhaps a soft rather than mechanical appearance could nonetheless render it less stigmatizing.

This epitomizes the contribution that designers could make to disability, bringing not only their skills but also the idiosyncrasies of their trains of thought. Breaking new ground demands new perspectives, and sometimes this comes from challenging the assumptions written into the brief itself. In this case size, for example, is not an absolute requirement but a means to the ends of creating a convenient and nonstigmatizing product. Good solutions to these higher issues may not necessarily be the smallest designs.

a little cough and a little lift

Azumi's work often involves what she terms *the enjoyment of transformation*, and so her thoughts return to folding step stools as she considers the particular needs of this brief and these people.

Azumi identifies two roles that the design of any folding mechanism on a step stool will inevitably serve. Both are hardly the criteria that would appear on a technical specification for a hinge, and illustrate a broader, more emotional, and social perspective, not just to the design as a whole, but even to details that would not normally be thought of in this way.

The first role she calls *a little cough*. Consider the situation in which a person with restricted growth is in a public environment—for instance, in a bar. If they wish to approach the bar to order a round of drinks, a step stool can help put them at a height where the bartender can see them and they can catch the bartender's eye. But if the bar is crowded, setting up the step stool requires a bit of space to do this in. The act of unfolding the steps can itself play a role in this negotiation. It becomes a little announcement to those around, even a performance—a perspective that echoes Azumi's interest and previous involvement with theater. And with any announcement, *tone of voice* is important. If the act is too discreet, it may go unnoticed; if too disturbing, it may have everyone in the room staring, and leave the person feeling stigmatized by the step stool. The mechanical design will, deliberately or inadvertently, determine this tone of voice.

maquettes on a bookshelf in Tomoko Azumi's studio

The second role Azumi calls *a little lift*. The person with restricted growth would obviously rather not have to carry around a step stool at all. However it is designed, this will be an inconvenience—one that the user could come to resent whatever its occasional benefits. So the moment they go to the additional trouble of unfolding it, the way this happens should be rewarding. Each time, it should give them a small emotional as well as a sufficient physical lift. Not in a loud way, not to attract attention as before, but for the satisfaction of the owner alone.

This joyous quality is shared by many of the designs featured in this book. Muji's CD player induces a smile whenever you tug on its cord. It is all part of an attention to detail that acknowledges that few aspects of a design are a purely technical or even ergonomic consideration. Our emotions are affected by the minutiae of our interactions with both the designed world and each other.

overleaf: Tomoko Azumi explores unfolding a step stool in a crowded bar

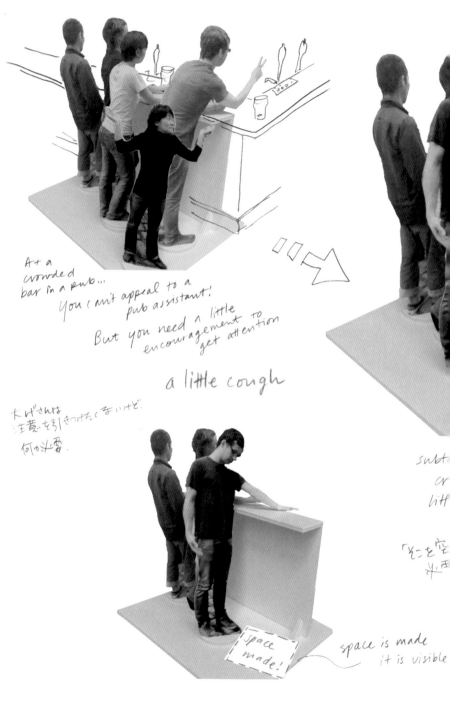

At a
crowded
bar in a pub...
You cant appeal to a
pub assistant!
But you need a little
encouragement to
get attention

a little cough

大げさには
注意を引きつけたくないけど!
何か必要.

subt
cr
litt

「そこを空
火,モ

space is made
it is visible

space
made!

wow!

open up!

Getting 'pleasant' attention
by elegant movement
(almost like an entertainment

this is important to
lift your mind a bit,
reduce hesitation of
getting attention

a little lift

「注意」を引きつけてしまうように/ふっと
心理的な負担を
軽くする。

open up

action

°°

ても
覚化できる.

Hello!

steps!

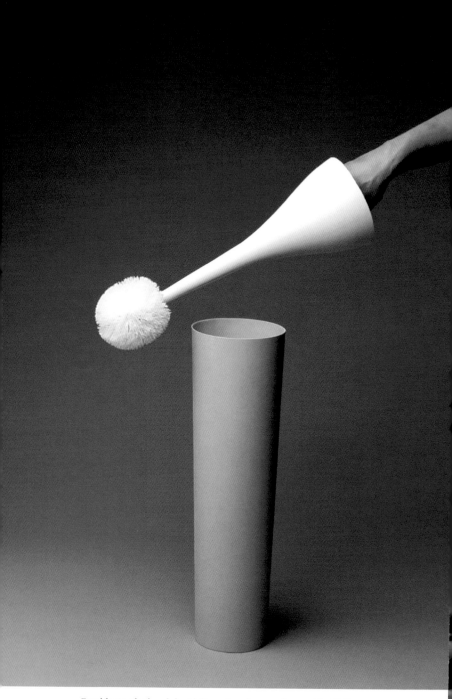

Excalibur toilet brush by Philippe Starck, manufactured by Heller

if Philippe Starck met bottom wipers

Many people have restricted reach that prevents them from carrying out basic toileting functions. For some of these using a bottom wiper, around which toilet paper is wrapped, can restore privacy. BIME has developed a folding bottom wiper that can be carried in a handbag or pocket, and this is a best seller for its manufacturing division.[1] The product has a tool-like appearance somewhat at odds with the intimacy of its use. When considering such a practical yet sensitive product, Starck may be a surprising candidate. Starck, the iconic designer of design icons, tends to polarize opinion among medical engineers. For some, his twenty-year-old Juicy Salif lemon squeezer epitomizes "style over function," and is used to dismiss designers as impractical and frivolous, even to question their role in a field as challenging and profound as design for disability.[2]

poetry in mundane products

Yet over the years Starck has consistently brought warmth, wit, and a certain poetry to the most mundane of household utensils: toothbrushes, flyswatters, and toilet brushes. He has remained as inspired by these everyday briefs as by the furniture and landmark hotels more expected of an international design star. Starck's toilet brush evokes a jousting lance in reference to the chivalrous task ahead. Perhaps there is even a place for quiet humor in a product designed to restore dignity—a wry smile for its user alone. Design for disability could be enriched by more of Starck's approach, not less.

Lotus swivel armchair by Jasper Morrison for Cappellini

if Jasper Morrison met wheelchairs

Wheelchairs support and transport people with a variety of disabilities, and so their design is always a challenging mix of clinical and technical demands. Mobility is the priority, but mobility is not everything; since people may sit in them all day, their wheelchairs will form part of other people's perception of them, an intimate association analogous to their clothing or the interior of their home. Given this cultural connection with the furniture that we select for our homes, it seems inappropriate not to invite the best furniture designers to contribute their skills and sensibilities to the design of wheelchairs too. Morrison is a furniture designer whose chairs grace art galleries and everyday homes. His pieces are often visually restrained, their simplicity belying their subtlety, yet nonetheless approachable and frequently sensual. Over time he has diversified into products and vehicles, carrying these values with him.

a wheelchair and chair collection

Morrison has designed furniture collections, with different chairs and stools united by a common design language. What about a furniture collection of wheelchairs and static chairs? How might each inspire the other? David Constantine from the wheelchair organization Motivation says that he can feel rather upright and somewhat detached when everyone else is lounging on sofas, and perhaps this even changes their perceptions of him too. How might shared furniture change everyone's experience of a shared evening?

recycled *Readymade* from found bicycle fork and electric components
designed by Marriott for the TEN project

Michael Marriott meets wheelchairs

RGK Interceptor wheelchair

wheelchairs

Wheelchairs have undergone a radical reinvention in the past decades, as described in **exploring meets solving**. Modern alloys and other materials have improved their lightness and maneuverability, and construction principles and components from bicycle design have otherwise transformed their performance and appearance. A ubiquitous mountain bike–like design language has emerged, partly out of the elements that the two products share these days, but also because this is a positive image, given the associations with fitness and capability. Certainly, they are more positive than the associations with hospitals—and by implication a *medical model* of disability—that upright, chromed, tubular steel wheelchairs still evoke.

This convergence of wheelchairs and mountain bikes could be challenged, however, and probably should be. It will not be to everyone's taste and culture, just as in our everyday lives we don't all choose to wear technically sophisticated outdoor clothing or footwear, whatever the practical benefits. Our tastes in clothing and furniture are often less practical, and usually more emotional.

Wheelchair design is so sophisticated these days, and one of the by-products of this is that it attracts and demands designers who are fluent in this technical sophistication. This will tend to perpetuate the current approach. Design progresses, in common with art and science, by challenging values that have become so widespread as to become assumptions. So the industry could really benefit from more people who are as fascinated with furniture as they are with bicycles.

There is one obvious problem of course: manual wheelchairs will continue to share lightweight wheels and other components with bikes. Adopting the design language of mountain bikes at least ensures a consistency, whereas any radical alternative might risk looking like a chair with bicycle wheels stuck on as an afterthought. But contrast need not mean incoherence.

XL1 Kit chair by Michael Marriott, his degree showpiece at the Royal
College of Art

Michael Marriott

Thinking about how wheelchairs might adopt a different design language while still retaining spoked wheels brought to mind the British furniture designer Michael Marriott. He often juxtaposes found objects and furniture: wooden spoons are appropriated as coat hooks, gym weights are recast as lamp bases or candlesticks, and bowling pins become the legs of coffee tables. Each object is at once recognizable out of context, yet well suited to these secondary purposes. There is frequently a slight awkwardness in these new compositions, but this seems to add to their charm.

Marriott's XL1 Kit chair has an informal aesthetic, halfway between a mass-produced and a low-cost handmade product. It is certainly different from the overt technical optimization of a sports wheelchair. His goal for this, his furniture design degree project at the Royal College of Art, was to be "comfortable, affordable, produce-able, friendly, honest and real furniture as opposed to irrelevant prototypes."[1] The reconciliation of *honest* and *friendly* is an interesting one. Marriott's work is pragmatic without being prosaic.

meeting

Marriott's work suggests the possibility of bringing new perspectives from the culture of furniture design to wheelchairs. Suppose the technical components of the modern wheelchair were retained but not the tubular alloy frame. Perhaps the spoked wheels could be juxtaposed with a quite different approach to the rest of the chair.

chairs meet bicycles

What I didn't realize was that bicycles are already something of an obsession for Marriott. On visiting his studio in an old factory in the East End of London, he shows me a small adjoining workshop in the roof space, with as many bicycles as chairs hanging from the beams, and spare wheels in the rafters.

chairs and wheelchairs hanging from the rafters in Marriott's
studio workshop

He points out an old folding bicycle and a damaged shopping bicycle from the 1970s, both with small wheels, that he intends to combine to make one good bike. The folding bicycle, a Moulton, has a tubular space-frame structure. Nearby is a chair with an equally, overtly structural frame, this time in cast aluminum: Chair_ONE by Konstantin Grcic, an industrial designer who initially trained as a cabinetmaker, and whose work has been variously described as discreet, elegant, and intense.

Alongside that is a battered old chair that he is fixing up, quite a rare design by the twentieth-century French designer Jean Prouvé, of whom Marriott has long been a fan. Prouvé was first apprenticed to a blacksmith and continued to explore the possibilities of sheet metal at a time when his modernist contemporaries had almost unanimously adopted tubular steel. Coincidentally Prouvé's workshop, Atelier Prouvé, manufactured bicycles during the Second World War. Bicycles to chairs and back to bicycles. Prouvé was as much an architect and engineer as a designer. Marriott thinks that he would have been a particularly interesting person to take on the design of a wheelchair because whatever he did involved a quite specific, often unconventional way of doing things.

He warms to the discussion: "Wheelchairs are midway between chairs and bicycles," he said, "my fascinations in life. I usually have a project involving at least one of the two going on at any one time."[2] He tells me that he is interested in the connections and gray areas between chairs and bicycles, and how this inevitably embraces wheelchairs. We briefly fantasize about furniture manufacturer Vitra branching into wheelchairs, and how its production processes and attention to detail could in itself influence their design.

Marriott has an artist friend who uses a wheelchair that he describes as a beautiful chair with a fine titanium steel frame. Despite costing several thousand pounds, these chairs only last him twelve to eighteen months before the front wheel bearings, which take an enormous amount of shock loading, wear

Part Number

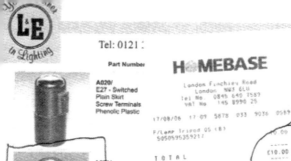

A020/
E27 - Switched
Plain Skirt
Screw Terminals
Phenolic Plastic

A025/
E27 - Switched
Half Thread Skirt
Screw Terminals
Phenolic Plastic

A027/
E27 - Switched
Full Thread Skirt
Screw Terminals
Phenolic Plastic

A028/
E27 - Plain Skirt
Screw Terminals
Thermosetting Plastic

A029/
E27 - Half Thread Skirt
Screw Terminals
Thermosetting Plastic

A030/
E27 - Full Thread Skirt
Screw Terminals
Thermosetting Plastic

A032/BLK
A032/WHT
A032/GLD
Shade Rings for
ES/BC Lampholders
Thermosetting Plastic

A036/BLK
A036/WHT
A036/GLD
Shade Rings for
ES/BC Lampholders
Thermosetting Plastic

/NIP
M10 Metal
Rotation ⋮

Order (Part Number)/(colour)/(tap):

/ASF
M10 Moulded Entry
/NIP
M10 Metal Entry with Anti-
Rotation Screw

montage of Marcel Duchamp influences and off-the-shelf electric
components from Michael Marriott's response to the TEN project

out. This gets Marriott back to Alex Moulton, the engineer who designed the Moulton folding bicycle. Moulton's background was as a suspension engineer who worked with Alec Issigonis on the Mini and later the hydrolastic suspension for the Austin 1100. Marriott seems to be looking for inspiration and association rather than deriving solutions from first principles. "What might Alex Moulton have done?" ironically seems a designer's thought, at the same time inclusively, appropriately blurring the distinction between design and engineering.

It starts to feel as though the conversation is coming full circle. Marriott seems more inspired by bicycles than furniture design, more inspired by engineers than designers as he argues that Moulton would be a much better wheelchair designer than he would be. But then I realize that although Marriott is reverential toward the kinds of engineers one might expect to be working on wheelchairs already, our conversation is still stirring up fresh perspectives. Being inspired as much by the engineer as their engineering, the reference points veer from analogous details to more diverse projects, and the trains of thought are more radical as a result.

if Alex Moulton had met Marcel Duchamp

What is exciting is that Marriott looks out from design in both directions, deriving inspiration as much from art as from engineering. In a recent project, TEN, he was one of ten designers invited by curator Chris Jackson to express a personal perspective on sustainable design issues, and to do this by creating an object from materials found within ten kilometers from their studio and with a budget of just ten pounds. His response was a lamp made from a wooden stool, a pair of bicycle forks, and a few domestic electric components. Chairs and bicycles again.

The piece is, of course, a homage to Duchamp's *Bicycle Wheel* of 1913, the artist's first influential *Readymade* (technically it is one of his *assisted readymades*, since the bicycle forks have been modified by upending and mounting on a stool). Duchamp later recalled that the original was created as a "distraction," a kinetic sculpture with a spinning wheel and rotating forks, and that he "enjoyed looking at it, just as I enjoy looking at the flames dancing in the fireplace," but its lasting importance is conceptual.[3] Beautiful as it is, the significance of the wheel is its ubiquity, and by proposing that any mass-produced object can become art, the piece was challenging the very definition of art and the artist. The *Readymades* have been described as a radical attempt to create antiart. Perhaps there is a role for antidesign in design for disability, a challenge to the technical tour de force. Ironic as this may sound, many designers are fascinated by antidesign. Design curator Clare Catterall noted in her introductory essay to *Specials*, a book about antidesign in graphic design, that "slick computer-generated design is now being tempered with a more human(e) aesthetic by way of a re-acquaintance with the awkwardness of manual operation."[4]

Likewise, new hybrids between bicycles and chairs could redefine the aesthetics of wheelchair design, but more important, could acquire a conceptual role too. Perhaps we are so wedded to the idea of the wheelchair as a finely engineered machine that we overlook a more obvious alternative: that a wheelchair might after all be a chair with wheels attached. Maybe this would seem like a technical step backward, but with the wheelchair so pivotal in representing disability as a whole, perhaps this degree of understatement might actually have some positive messages.

In this context, what is therefore exciting about Marriott is his tendency to be thinking of Moulton *and* Duchamp as well as Prouvé and Grcic, to be thinking of chairs as well as bicycles, and taking inspiration across the spectrum from art to craft and furniture design, industrial design, manufacturing, and engineering. The spirit is interdisciplinary rather than multidisciplinary, illustrating the cross-fertilization that occurs within design as well as between design and other disciplines.

tiered wooden skirt from Hussein Chalayan's Autumn/Winter 2000 collection

if Hussein Chalayan met robot arms

Medical engineers are applying robotics to the needs of people with little or no movement of their own arms.[1] Along with the technology, these robot arms have adopted the design language of light industrial robots, with protective outer casings or fabric sleeves. Exploring radical alternatives is not part of the priorities or skills of the current development teams. Fashion design could have so much to contribute, since a sleeve is designed to flex and flow, whereas the form of most products is static. "Clothes acquire another sense of life in movement," says Hussein Chalayan, one of the most experimental of fashion designers, whose work is characterized by the inventive use of materials and cut.[2]

conceptual not literal

Yet Chalayan's work is at the same time highly conceptual; it is frequently metaphoric rather than literal. Speaking about his famed Autumn/Winter 2000 collection, in which tables and chairs transformed into clothing, including a polished wooden coffee table that became a tiered wooden skirt, he stressed that "the project had nothing to do with furniture. It was all about the moment of trying to leave your home at a time of war."[3] Here is a dilemma: that Chalayan has the skills to transform the design of any robot arm, but that adopting a more conceptual approach could be more valuable still. The influence of a designer like Chalayan could be as much in exploring the very idea of a robot arm, the idea of assistive technology, as in determining its actual, final design. We need both influences.

concept eyewear for Eastman by Martin Bone exploring new
applications for cellulose acetate and other thermoplastics

Martin Bone meets prosthetic legs

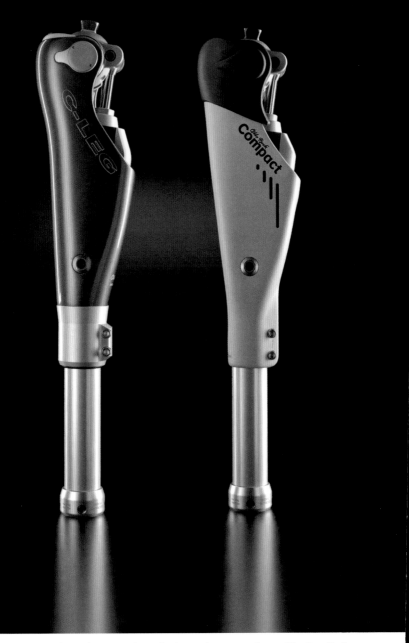

C-leg and Compact lower limb prostheses manufactured by Otto Bock

prosthetic legs

Whether prosthetic legs are passive or powered, their aesthetics tend to follow one of two principles: *cosmetic* legs are visual replicas of human limbs, while the appearance of *functional* prostheses derives directly from their structural and mechanical components.

The materials with which cosmetic legs are covered are therefore chosen for their visual resemblance to human skin, whereas functional prostheses are not so much designed as exposed: it is the absence of a cosmetic cover that defines them, revealing skeletal and muscular materials selected for their mechanical properties. Hugh Herr at the MIT Media Lab wears prostheses of this latter type, appreciating the elegance, efficiency, and honesty of mechanical engineering, but this is not to the taste of many amputees. Some amputees are also uncomfortable with cosmetic limbs, which they may think macabre or *fake*, or just not like the *feel* of, because when prosthetic limbs are designed to imitate the look of human skin, their tactile qualities may be overlooked.

This leaves a large gap between these two extremes. What about a third approach, which would not mimic the human leg but be inspired by a strong, considered aesthetic? Aimee Mullins has modeled in beautiful but eerie glass legs, but this is an exception. What materials might be chosen for prosthetic legs neither for their resemblance to human skin nor entirely for their mechanical properties?

Martin Bone

Martin Bone is an industrial designer at IDEO, where he works with others on a diversity of products, including televisions and computers, pens and PDAs, each a balance between desire and practicality.

He is inspired by the inherent aesthetic qualities of materials, or what designers refer to as *materiality*. Rather than considering the form first, and applying surfaces and finishes second,

IDEO TechBox collection of inspiring materials samples

as many designers do, it is as if he designs outward from the materials themselves, choosing them for their character and then expressing this further through their eventual form. "I'm always focused on materials. Materials are the source of inspiration," says Bone, "because they are a way for the user to connect to the object."[1]

This focus occasionally attracts projects in which materials are written into the brief. Bone led a project for Eastman, which wanted to revive interest among manufacturers and designers in its range of thermoplastics, such as cellulose acetate, which is made from tree sap (and from which the original Lego bricks were made in 1949). With materials specialist Kara Johnson and others, Bone created a contemporary range of eyewear inspired by these "forgotten materials."[2]

His own concept was a radical pair of sunglasses that wrapped around the back of the head rather than sitting on the wearer's nose bridge. The idea was that the person would have her head geometrically scanned when she went to the optician, and then not only would the lenses be to her prescription but so would the frames. A laminated construction suited the idea of each pair being made to order, and Bone then experimented with combining cellulose acetate in different colors with other materials with complementary properties. He tried sandwiching the thermoplastic between hardwood— interesting because this is the source material for the plastic— and copper. Bone described copper as something of a personal obsession. "Copper patinas beautifully and I love the idea of the glasses getting older as the wearer ages."[3] These three traditional materials combine to make a radical composite.

meeting

What equally radical approaches might be employed in prosthetic legs? As soon as we start our first conversation about this, I am struck by how natural it is to apply Bone's approach. He engages with this medical product in the same way that I

experimental lamination of wood, copper, and acrylic

have heard him discuss any other, if anything with an added enthusiasm inspired not by the importance of this brief but by its intimacy.

Bone's first thought is how sensual the body is and what it would mean to create designs from this perspective. Rather than to replicate the look of a human limb, what about creating something that has its own inherent sensuality?

the materiality of men's and women's legs

Sensuality leads to sexuality, and obviously men's legs are different from women's. Can the materials represent these differences? What about a polished wood or smooth ceramic for women—strength without the coldness of metal? What about felt for men—roughness and a degree of softness combined?

Bone is at pains to point out that he is not advocating a return to old-fashioned wooden legs or rejecting the technology of modern prosthetics. But he wonders whether we could build more sensuality into lightweight structural materials by creating new composites, lest we lose the interesting nature of materials that are too heavy to use on their own. Could we create composite veneers, he asks, such as a carbon fiber substrate with an oak overlay? He envisions an appropriate balance of the human-made with the natural, the calculated geometry of carbon fiber with the organic variability of wood grain.

bespoke legs

The uniqueness of samples of certain materials leads the conversation to the uniqueness of people themselves. The added benefit of using laminates for the Eastman eyeglasses was that the wearer could choose his own combination of materials. Bone's inspiration was the tailored suit, and it does seem inappropriate that the same degree of personal choice and expression does not apply to prosthetic limbs, which may be clinically customized but are aesthetically off-the-shelf. When I ask what materials he could imagine amputees specifying, given the choice, Bone is intrigued by choices as weird as Astroturf or glass. "Maybe the only hard constraint should be sheet materials that can be formed."[4]

What, then, would be the role of the designer? Bone sees the designer/maker, like the tailor, as a *curator* of all this choice. He would tell you what will work and what might not, visually as well as technically. He would have samples for the customer to experiment with (a territory that I explored myself at the Royal College of Art through the design of a bespoke prosthetic hand) and the equipment, the presses, to make the laminates. It is likely that different people would make this choice for different reasons, against different criteria—racial, aesthetic, or cultural. How much more expressive this would be than just "matching" skin color. This goes so much further than just the physical differences between people.

The Open Source Prosthetics movement is challenging the model of clinical prescription within a hospital setting, substituting this for one of the private workshop. An episode called "Pimp my gimp" in the newspaper cartoon strip *Doonesbury* portrayed amputees getting custom paint jobs in automotive body shops. Healthy though these challenges are, perhaps there is a danger of reverting to the *garden shed* model of a lone inventor undercutting the prosthetics industry, an amateur needing considerable technical skills, so perhaps not equally motivated by, or fluent in, the issues we are discussing here.

Bone finds himself more inspired by the contemporary rediscovery and reinvention of traditional craft and "punk manufacturing" among young people. He's seen amputees with tattooed prosthetics that exude attitude and provocation. But he doesn't think that this necessarily means people doing it themselves. "It's still about skilled craftspeople, including the people who create the legs today. After all I don't want to make the suit. I want my tailor to: someone with better skills and a better eye than me. I don't want to work out the mechanism because this would then become my focus, and most of the stuff in this area is already about the mechanism not the aesthetics."[5] A partnership of prosthetist, amputee, and designer could together create what none of them could develop on their own.

men versus women; Shimano versus Campagnolo

Returning to the idea of a difference between men's and women's prostheses, Bone makes the analogy to Shimano versus Campagnolo bicycle parts. "Both take very different approaches to the same problem. One is engineered and masculine, the other sensual and strong. Some Campagnolo castings are beautifully organic. The vintage ones are really stunning."[6] So the essence of masculinity or femininity could be embodied in a combination of materials and form. It's a fascinating analogy, and adds another layer of nuance to the discussion of wheelchairs and bicycles: the issue of whether we should use bike parts depends on which parts we are talking about. Bone notices these overlooked differences, and once pointed out, their relevance is clear. It's just another illustration of why designers should be involved in the earliest and broadest conversations about assistive technology.

abstracting skin, muscle, and bone

We become intrigued by the idea of relinquishing visual imitation without abandoning a reference to the feel of the human body. This implies abstraction: materials that may not feel exactly like skin but that have some of its qualities, or might be pleasant to touch in their own right. Bone is inspired by the aesthetic relationship between the structure and cover of a prosthesis, inspired to play with the contrast between hard and soft, skeleton and tissue.

He pursues the idea of using soft materials like felt, and stamping patterns into the felt so that it flexes and responds when touched, and then also reveals parts of the mechanism beneath. At this point on a live project, he would start making sketch prototypes with material samples just to get a sense of how it could be to feel the mechanism through the felt, like muscle beneath skin. Rather than having the mechanism exposed, this could indirectly convey the strength and technical sophistication within. "I can imagine a carbon fiber substrate that has cutaway elements. The soft material is wrapped over the top, and covers the open and the hard areas. As you feel your way around the leg, the perception changes much like if you feel your way around from your shin to calf."[7] Bone explores this further on the next pages.

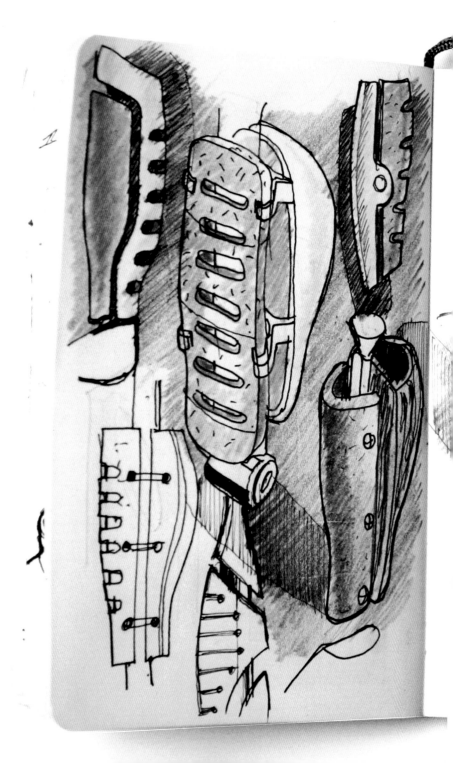

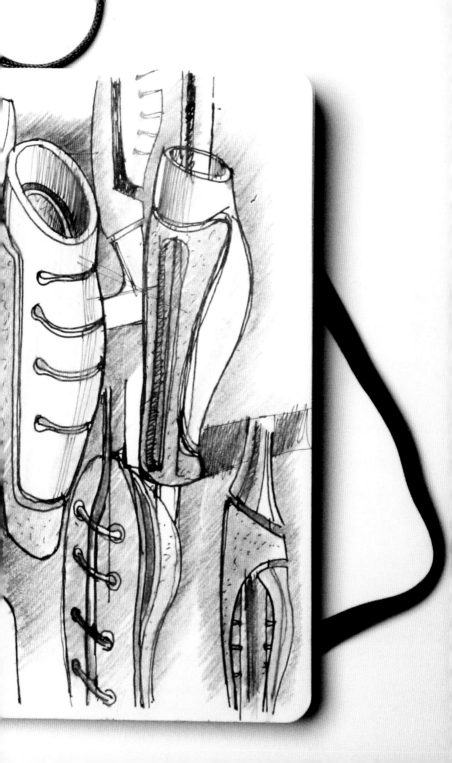

iPod earphones by Jonathan Ive's industrial design group at Apple

if Jonathan Ive met hearing aids

For some in the hearing aid industry, wireless cell phone earpieces point to an exciting future: similar devices, worn by people without hearing impairments. But often these products do not wear their technology lightly, with silver moldings and flashing blue LEDs, and outside a predominantly male market of early adopters, this can be stigmatizing in its own way. Jonathan Ive leads Apple's industrial design team, responsible for humanizing so many high-tech products and giving them a subtler appeal. Wireless or not, Apple's signature white iPod earphones represent an alternative ideal. A teenager I saw using a white hearing aid, which was more visible from a distance than a flesh-pink one, looked self-confident wearing it.

establishing a design language

But Apple's appeal is not contained in a color. Just as the first iMac spawned a plague of inept translucent imitations, so there was no mistaking this white hearing aid for a new Apple product. In detail, no white is pure white, and this makes a difference, as do the color and texture of this printed page. More important, any design language exists in the whole as well as the details. Apple products use a broad but carefully chosen family of materials and finishes—metals, plastics, and elastomers; white, black, silver, or colored; self-colored, back painted, or transparent; polished, etched, or anodized—yet each product is recognizable even without the logo. How would Ive approach the remarkable technology in a hearing aid? What might an Apple iEar look like, and feel like?

detail of *The Willoughby* suit by Paul Smith, showing the intriguing lining that only its wearer may see

if Paul Smith met hearing aids

Hearing aids are designed to be heard and not seen. Traditionally, this has implied flesh-colored plastic, for camouflage against the skin. This is then extended to the whole of the device, perhaps to reduce the parts count, or perhaps for lack of a reason to do otherwise. Leaving aside the external appearance of a hearing aid, why couldn't the parts *not* seen by others be given a quite different treatment? What if those surfaces of a hearing aid that fitted into the ear were beautifully, even extravagantly detailed?

attention to hidden details

Fashion designer Paul Smith pays as much attention to what the wearer of his clothing notices as to what everyone else sees. The wearer's experience has already begun when they reach for the clothes hanger, hold the fabric, and fasten the buttons. Labels, lining, hemming, and in Smith's case flashes of his trademark multicolored stripes are carefully, sometimes wittily applied, although invisible to all but intimate acquaintances. But the wearer knows that they are there, and they make the clothes feel different and the wearer feel special. Whether a person decides to display or conceal her disability—and the designs of devices and prostheses should be enabling a choice of such expression—perhaps there is a separate issue of feeling comfortable in private. Rituals of use become part of the fabric of our lives. Those unseen details—a cleaning cloth, or a box that hearing aids might be put into at night—are all part of that experience.

Cutler and Gross flagship store in London's Knightsbridge

if Cutler and Gross met hearing aids

If the design of hearing aids remains medical, then so has the way in which they are purchased. While it is now possible to visit a store rather than a clinic, the experience is more one of prescription than of consumerism. Hearing aid shops today have much in common with opticians thirty years ago. Tony Gross, cofounder of Cutler and Gross, is a trained optometrist himself, but as early as the 1960s started to see the irony of optometrists themselves selling glasses. "It was as if you visited a chiropodist and when he had finished treating your feet, he expected to help you choose a pair of fashionable shoes. Yet that was the service that opticians were offering and that many still are."[1] And to a large extent that is how hearing aids are still retailed.

fashion retail for fashionable hearing aids

More recently, Gross has also established a vintage sunglasses store within the Comme des Garçons Dover Street Market (DSM). Rei Kawakubo created DSM as an eclectic mix of independent fashion designers and other unexpected retailers. (The Cutler and Gross store is not an optician, but prescription lenses can be fitted elsewhere.) Would Comme des Garçons ever consider a suitably edgy hearing aid store? If so, what might a DSM hearing aid concession look like? Could this help change perceptions of hearing aids and hearing impairment a little? And returning to the importance of the culture of deafness, might this appeal first to people who are Deaf with a capital D or deaf with a little d?

MeBox storage with perforated dots that can be punched out to create letters or icons, designed and manufactured by GTF

Graphic Thought Facility meets braille

14 steps to your perfect latte...

Grind, **dose**, **tam** then **tap**, **twist**, **wipe** and **lock**.

Push, **purge**, **stretch** and **swirl**.

Tap, **pour** and **ser**

...ready for you to sip and enjoy!

interior of Café Revive designed by GTF

braille signage

The presence of braille in a public space sets up some intriguing contradictions. It can be invaluable to braille readers, but these are only a minority of blind people, so braille is only ever one part of making a space accessible to a wide range of visually impaired people. At the same time, its very illegibility to sighted people can make it more conspicuous, and more evocative of disability than many other accessibility measures that may go unnoticed. Braille has an iconic presence.

Yet braille is seldom found in the design brief for signage and other graphics, often being treated as a separate accessibility issue and even being implemented by a different team. We have all been in buildings where braille has quite clearly been applied as an afterthought: on separate plates, in different materials, at a different time to other signage. Usually it does not relate to the rest of the interior, and frequently it visually detracts from it. Perhaps this treatment is because braille is only seen as a legal obligation, a necessary compromise. Or perhaps it is considered too specialized an issue for architects and interior and graphic designers to be involved with. Either way, this marginalization is likely to limit braille to an absolute legal minimum, a visible sign of this attitude toward accessibility in general.

It also just seems a missed opportunity. Braille is interesting and beautiful, as abstract visual and tactile decoration, intriguing and indecipherable to the nonreader, like cuneiform or Linear B. It must be possible for braille to inspire, not always compromise, an environment.

Graphic Thought Facility

The work of the design consultancy GTF includes interiors, exhibitions, products, and books. It has designed information graphics for London's Science Museum and the Design Museum. In a café interior, a map of the world taking up an entire wall resolves into flower patterns as you approach it,

sprinkled chocolate wall decoration in Café Revive

each of which is further revealed to be made of sprinkled chocolate. GTF also works in print, on beautiful books with exquisite details.

meeting

It is partly this range of scale that makes me think that GTF might be inspired by braille and take an innovative approach to it. Braille has dimensions of a few millimeters, and of course needs to be read within arm's length, so using it within interiors requires thinking about the design at a distance and close up.

Running through GTF's graphic design is a strong feeling for materials and production techniques, and the visual languages that they can support. Braille's precision and unalterable structure lends it something of the nature of a material, or a production process to be applied to a material. GTF's work is an imaginative and thoughtful mix of high-tech and low-tech, of custom electroluminescent displays and traditional printing techniques. "We are always on the lookout for slightly obscure printing and production techniques that are fit for their original purpose, but that can lend them to also be appropriate in another context," says Andy Stevens, one of three directors at GTF. "But we are wary of innovation for novelty's sake, though: the process has to be apt."[1] Sometimes this is at a detailed level of different weights of card and board. At other times it involves taking materials from one industry and applying them to another.

Perhaps most important of all, tactile as well as visual qualities are crucial to GTF. Designing the visually beautiful book of Tord Boontje's work written by Martina Margetts for Rizzoli, GTF took a technique of punching that Boontje had applied to metal furniture and used it with paper, creating a precious, braille-like texture to the pages and a subtle resistance when separating the pages from one another. The perforations are also there for a graphic reason, however: the large page sizes that show the commissioned photography to such effect are rather too large to fill with text, so the texture balances this

perforated page in *Tord Boontje*, published by Rizzoli, and inspired by

Boontje's own furniture and lighting

without eliminating white space. It was not a simple step, but took many tests and trials getting it to work with the printer, even though it involved reusing an existing process. The use of scrim on the front cover gives the book a nice feel in the hand and a certain sense of fragility. This material is part of the bookmaking process anyway, only normally quite hidden. "Bringing it to the surface seemed quite Tord-like," remarks Stevens, "playing games with inside and outside."[2]

GTF's own MeBox is a storage box made from cardboard that is screen printed different colors on each side and then folded over on itself. When the perforated dots on the outside wall are punched out, the contrasting color on the cardboard wall behind shows through. In this way its owner can create text, icons, or patterns on a dot matrix grid. The resulting labeling gives lots of freedom, but with a strong visual language, however it is used. Perhaps braille could be approached in a similar way, as much as a material or a production process than as a text? If braille signage were more easily composed and even rewritten, for example, how might this inspire new content and new uses?

Although GTF has been involved with signage for public spaces like museums in which accessibility was part of the overall program, braille has never formed part of its brief, but something that a different team was responsible for on an entirely separate project. Talking with Stevens and fellow director Huw Morgan, they both say that they would have relished being asked to think about braille and other accessibility. They have actually been intrigued by braille for a while, they explain.

braille as a material

Around its studio, GTF has hundreds of samples of different materials. As students at the Royal College of Art, where they first met, Stevens remembers that they were always in the materials library, a collection of inspiring materials samples and manufacturers' brochures aimed at architecture and industrial

tiles by Lubna Chowdhary

design students—disciplines that usually work with raw materials. Stevens recalls the selection of laminates in particular, from the bizarre to the mundane, that could evoke moods and associations, from futurism to school days.

Among GTF's samples, Morgan locates a tactile map of the British Isles produced by the RNIB. The embossing on the braille map is impressive, and GTF takes pleasure in rediscovering a technique or material that has been passed over or forgotten. For the Stealing Beauty exhibition of young British designers at the Institute of Contemporary Arts in London, GTF revived the technique of routing into laminated colored and white plastic, traditionally used for name badges and door signs, playing with the contradictions of traditional and contemporary, designed and mundane. Stevens describes similar exciting contradictions in braille: "It's got a ticker-tape aesthetic. It's space writing. It has a futuristic system-ness but at the same time is old-fashioned."[3]

The RNIB map is an embossed outline of the coastline, with a texture representing the sea and braille place-names corresponding to the positions of cities on the land. Stevens is fascinated by it. "On one level it is so stark, so 'crude,' as a piece of graphic design, if it can be called that. It is lovely to touch and hold, but the way that it is laid out is not elegant for sighted people."[4] He wonders whether elegance, and in what sense, is an issue for the blind people who read it. That takes us into a discussion of what is seen and not seen, and the thought that braille could be decorative for sighted people.

In an illustration of how GTF thought progresses, Stevens reaches for another box under his desk, this time containing a selection of beautiful ceramic tiles created by Lubna Chowdhary. The tiles were commissioned for a book that GTF designed for Nokia to launch a new range of phones with different finishes—leather, embossing, and etching. Chowdhary produced tiles with specific color palettes and textures, which were photographed in detail to complement the phones.

blowing up braille

Stevens and Morgan lay the tiles out on a bench and start to play with them. They imagine combining them in a grid to make a frieze. Their counterintuitive leap is to begin to think of the tiles as individual dots on a blown up—and therefore illegible—braille wall. Raised bumps could be represented by highly textured, patterned, and colored tiles; "empty" braille cells could be smooth, plain, and paler tiles. From a distance a visual representation of braille could be perceived, if not deciphered. The textures would also reflect light differently, so this might be revealed or hidden with changes in illumination. These are the games that graphic designers play with type after all, using it sometimes for decoration rather than meaning, and not always for both at once.

Close up, to a sighted or nonsighted audience, the contrast in textures between the rough and smooth tiles could be intriguing. The smooth tiles could actually carry information in braille, and lots of it—potentially far more than basic signage. What else might they say? The earliest manifestation of these ideas is illustrated on the pages that follow.

This leaves the unusual question of how visible type might relate to braille at different scales. How strange to be thinking about braille first and visible text second for a change. This is just a train of thought, of course, and it would need grounding in a specific brief before it could go much further. But this is an inspiring direction from which to approach signage; it feels as though we might even be on the cusp of thinking about visible text in a new way as a result.

overleaf: GTF conceives a wall of braille with sighted people and
visually impaired people in mind

Shops ←

Screen 1. →

Restaurant →

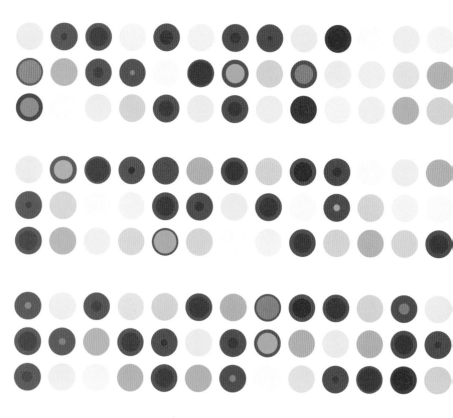

Ceramic tiles with areas of relief
provide rich decoration for
public areas as well as being
able to convey information in Braille.

Garland lamp shade by Tord Boontje

if Tord Boontje met braille

In accessible environments and public spaces, braille is not only a source of information for its readers (a small proportion of blind people) but also part of the visual experience of sighted people and the tactile experience of everyone. But often, as noted earlier, braille is obviously an afterthought, a result of directly solving the problems of accessibility, added on as separate pieces of material with little thought for the overall composition. Is this the aspiration of inclusive design? Yet why shouldn't this added medium and the new constraints it brings lead to new visual languages that might be appreciated by sighted people too? Braille's very abstractness and indecipherability lends it intrigue and beauty after all. Perhaps more playful and open-ended experimentation is required.

decoration as essence

Tord Boontje is a designer whose work is inspired by what might be termed *decoration*, yet with decorative detail as its essence rather than something applied. Most famously his Garland lamp shade is nothing but its delicate metal flowers. What might braille become in the hands of Boontje? How might it acquire a presence of its own, and a new relationship with a product or an environment? How might a braille reader's experience of the space be transformed, and if braille information exceeded conventional signage, how might this change the relationship between blind and sighted people in such a space?

The Accurate from Mr Jones Watches by Crispin Jones

Crispin Jones meets watches for
visually impaired people

watch made by Daniel Quare around 1700 that repeats the quarters
when the pendant is held down

watches for visually impaired people

For visually impaired people who cannot read a watch face, there are tactile or auditory alternatives. Each kind has a rich history; the first tactile watch was made in the eighteenth century. Present-day tactile watches usually have a pair of watch hands protected by a flip-up glass front. There are even historical examples of mechanical braille or braille-like displays—effectively the first ever digital watches. Electronic tactile watches include Tissot's Silen-T, described in **identity meets ability,** which combines touch pad technology and vibration feedback to create virtual hands.

The first audible watches were *repeaters*, developed in the seventeenth and eighteenth centuries, that imitated church bells by chiming the hours and quarters. *Minute repeaters* also chimed every minute, while a *Grande Sonnerie* sounded the hours, quarters, and minutes, or could be silenced and sound only on demand. Repeaters were not in fact designed primarily for blind people but also could help anyone tell the time by night before the invention of luminous hands or electric light, although they were just as much objects of desire as practicality. There were even tactile variants, *à tact* watches, in which "hammer and bell are replaced by a sharp pin which protrudes from the case to prick the finger once for each hour."[1]

A modern variant of this is a vibrating watch from the RNIB that reads out the time through a sequence of long and short pulses. For example, two long pulses (for p.m.) followed by three short pulses, one long pulse, and five short pulses represent a quarter past three in the afternoon.

The history of watches for blind people is inseparable from the history of watchmaking, but that relationship has all but been lost. Today, talking watches that play recorded or synthesized speech have little of the quality and qualities of contemporary watches. One RNIB vibrating watch is not even a wristwatch but a small box of electronics worn on the belt, and it looks more like a pager or smoke detector than a watch.

The Humility Watch, one of the original *Mr Jones Watches*, revives the tradition of the memento mori

Each tells the time, yet ignores that watches also convey other information to their wearer and others. Watches are not just functional instruments but play a role akin to our clothing and jewelry as well. The apparent value, conspicuousness, and accuracy of our watch may signal our wealth, chutzpah, and exactitude, or perhaps betray our avarice, pretentiousness, and pedantry.

Crispin Jones

Crispin Jones is an artist and designer whose work has considered the watch in particular and the representation of time in general. Mr Jones Watches was a critical design project in which he created a series of seven radical wristwatches, each of which in some way challenged the relationship between this intimate piece of technology and its wearer. Telling the time is only one part of a watch's role. Advertising impresses on us the need to impress others by brandishing our watch as a status symbol: "It's your watch that says most about who you are," claims Seiko.[2]

Jones was just as interested in the role a watch plays in its wearer's self-image, and how glancing at a watch hundreds of times every day might influence this obviously or subconsciously. He played with the principle of autosuggestion: that through the repetition of affirmative statements, such as "Day by day, in every way, I'm getting better and better," one might change one's personality. So The Personality Watch delivers the time along with an additional message, either positive "You are an amazing person | Twelve-fifty-two," or negative "All your friends hate you | Nine-fifty-five." Over time, these bring about a change in the wearer's personality. More extreme still, The Humility Watch revives the tradition of the memento mori, an object to remind people that they should be prepared for death at any moment. It does this with a mirrored display that alternates telling the time with the statement "Remember you will die." In this way, says Jones, over time it fosters humility in the wearer—a different role for a watch.

washing machine time displayed on *Fluidtime*, by Crispin Jones and
Michael Kieslinger at Interaction Design Institute Ivrea

meeting

When Jones and I start talking about watches for visually impaired people, we realize there are a number of directions that the conversation can follow. Most literally, talking watches could become versions of The Personality Watch or The Humility Watch by interjecting whispered subversive statements. This could be even more provocative coming from what many would describe as *assistive technology*. Perhaps even a critique of assistive technology, with its connotations of benevolence?

Returning to their role as a status symbol, watches for visually impaired people could do a lot more than they do to produce an inner glow for the wearer. A tactile watch should feel great to wear and read by touch. One might expect an attention to the warmth and weight of materials as well as the texture of finishes that even surpassed that of mainstream watches. And how might it impress other blind people? A watch strap that makes the gentlest of sounds whenever the wrist is flexed? Perhaps a subtle hint of sandalwood each time a talking watch is held to the ear? There is a danger here of reverting to the stereotype of blind people being particularly sensitive to smell parodied on the BlindKiss website, but watches for visually impaired people could communicate so much more, whereas at the moment they largely signal "I am blind."

critical design and blindness

Although initially a critical design project for publication and exhibition, Mr Jones Watches are now available as a limited edition series. So individual purchasers can choose to wear a more *critical* statement about his or her own attitudes toward watch design.

Building on the spirit of the BlindKiss website, which parodies certain attitudes toward blindness, could provocative watches allow visually impaired people to express something of their own attitude toward their disability or undermine other people's perceptions of this? Jones is intrigued by this, but declares himself "not comfortable that [he has] things to articulate about the experience of blind users."[3] This is a project he would only want to do together with visually impaired people.

time in the background

Jones is keen to get back to the fundamentals of telling the time. One significant difference between a visible watch and a tactile or auditory one is that you might notice the time "out of the corner of your eye."

Jones and sound and interaction designer Michael Kieslinger produced a series of more peripheral timepieces at the Interaction Design Institute in Ivrea, Italy. In *Fluidtime*, the movement of an abstract object on the wall of the design studio reflected the progress of a communal washing machine in the laundry block—meaningful if you knew what to look for, but otherwise discreet. Only when the washing cycle had finished and the machine was free for the next person to use did the display unfurl an array of bright blue ribbons. It was "designed to be unobtrusive until it had significant information to impart," and in this way it worked well in the background of an architectural space.[4]

A glance at a watch is quite different than flipping the lid of a tactile watch and interrogating it. In *The Discretion Watch* described in **identity meets ability,** we explored a tactile watch that would respond to languid body movements. This time, Jones is interested in an audible watch that might not rely on speech.

Jones divides his time between London and Tokyo, where he has worked with Japanese manufacturers on commercial projects. He is reminded of the Tokyo Metro's Yamanote line, a loop around central Tokyo, not unlike the Circle line on the London Underground. At each of its twenty-nine stations, a tune specific to that station is played inside the carriages. If commuters aren't paying attention to the spoken announcements, the familiar tune of their station is more likely to awake them from their thoughts. The circular line and the tunes get Jones thinking about whether a 'tune' could convey the time audibly, a rhythm playing out the position of hour and second hands on a sweep around the clock face. At twelve o'clock, the sounds representing the number twelve, the minute hand, and hour hand would all coincide as a three-note chord, whereas at 8:20 the three sounds would be played out as a triplet. Perhaps these sounds could play whenever the wearer shook his wrist, whether intentionally or not. This gesture would be more akin to pulling back a shirt cuff to look at a watch than to pressing a button on a talking watch.

precision and personality

So far, the idea still feels like an invention, not unlike the RNIB vibrating watch, rather than a piece of design, critical or otherwise. But it starts to reconnect with the issues of image and self-image once Jones goes into more detail. He is concerned about how accurately people would be able to judge the intervals between the hands. One way of increasing the legibility is to include intermediate audible markers. These are directly analogous to the markings on a watch face—whether just on the hour, on each quarter, every five minutes, every minute, or finer still. On a visible watch, minute gradations and below become as much about conveying the *idea* of accuracy as contributing to actual accuracy (or perhaps supporting the use of a second hand—but is the role of the second hand itself to tell the time with precision, to use as a stopwatch, to reassure us that the watch is still going, or is it aesthetic? What about a smooth sweeping second hand as opposed to one that indexes second by second, or half-second by half-second?).

On the following page, Jones maps these alternative visual markings onto the sounds made by the concept for sonic time. What *personalities* are implied by each sound? Which might appeal to whom?

overleaf: Crispin Jones maps out escalating accuracies of audible watches for diverse visually impaired people

Super minimal time information. May be difficult to interpret accurately, but then so is the Movado watch upon which it is based (is that 1:15 or 2:15?).

Basic simplified display - the markers on the hours are mapped.

Improved simplified display - markers on the hours are mapped but now there is differentiation the 12, 3, 6, and 9 o'clock mar

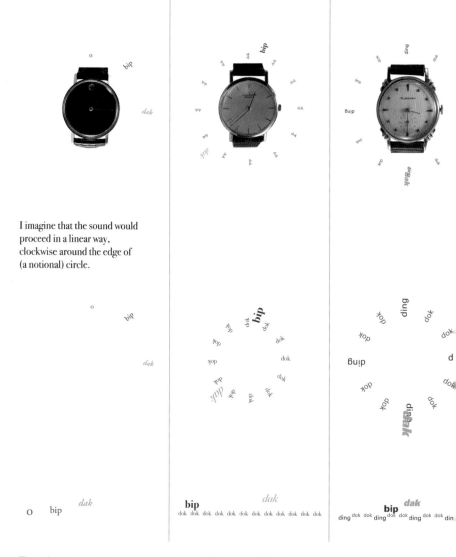

I imagine that the sound would proceed in a linear way, clockwise around the edge of (a notional) circle.

These drawings are a first pass at mapping some different watch displays to sonic information.
The sonic version is indicated visually with onomatopoeic words.

display - every minute is mapped,
e is differentiation on the hour
cators as well. The seconds are
ped as well.

Flashy display - every minute is mapped
and sub-divided into thirds as well,
There is differentiation on the hour
indicators and on the 12, 3, 6 and 9
o'clock markers.
The seconds are mapped as well.

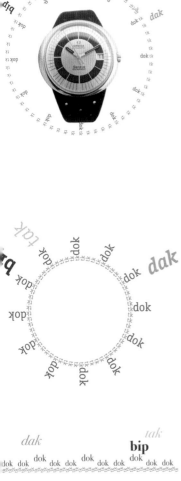

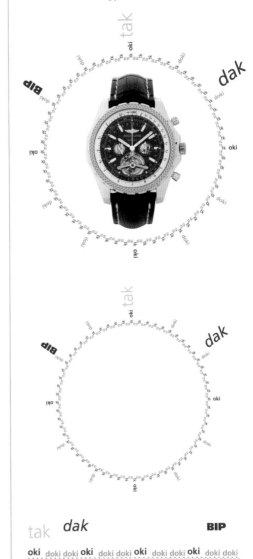

message wall for O2 by Durrell Bishop and Tom Hulbert at IDEO

if Durrell Bishop met communication aids

The Lightwriter is a well-respected communication aid manufactured by Toby Churchill, who is himself speech impaired. The product produces synthetic speech, but also has a text display facing the person being conversed with, thereby helping with intelligibility. This display is an off-the-shelf electronics component of the sort found in an office telephone or credit card machine, which seems at odds with the intimacy of these "spoken" words. The letters appear as soon as they are typed or selected—a functional by-product of the text entry, rather than a communication medium in its own right. A designer like Durrell Bishop, whose work blurs the boundaries between industrial design and interaction design, might help a company as sensitive as Toby Churchill go further.

text as the essence of a design

Bishop's work demonstrates a fascination with text, whether on the scale of a cell phone, a hat, or a three-story wall. He explores the way in which a flow of text, its choreography as much as its typography, can become the essence of a design, not just something that appears within a window or on a screen. Bishop and other interaction designers are bringing fresh perspectives to electronic media, and experimenting with new design languages that are appropriately unlike anything before them, but nonetheless have something of the warmth of printed and physical objects. In the case of communication aids, one might extend these qualities to the personal and individual, like handwriting, or to the emotional, like tone of voice.

bit.fall (2001–2005) by Julius Popp; view of installation in Paris in 2005,
160 cm, water, pump, magnetic valves, and electronic circuits

if Julius Popp met communication aids

If communication aids could employ far more imaginative and appropriate text displays, then these need not be restricted to LCD or LED technologies. Experimental displays have been created using ferrofluids shaped by magnetic fields, phosphorescent paint excited by ultraviolet light, or even modulated flames. This degree of invention might seem gratuitous for an advertising billboard, but surely a person's "speech" is precious enough to justify a magical expression. Bit.fall is an installation by German artist/designer Julius Popp. An array of solenoid valves open and close the flow of water from hundreds of jets, creating a succession of lines of "pixels," which then free-fall and can be read for an instant. The work is on an architectural scale, but speech too can fill a room or space.

speech is ephemeral

To see bit.fall as a new display technology is to misread it, however, and Popp has refused offers to license it for commercial purposes. It is an installation in which the medium was conceived in relation to the content it displays. Bit.fall samples current keywords from Internet news feeds and displays them as so much information running through our fingers. As soon as each line is created, it is falling, degrading, and dying, the water recycled for the next words. This is its greater message. Speech too is ephemeral, and this is part of its preciousness rather than a limitation. In this and other ways speaking is different from writing, so maybe it should be given visual expression in a different way too.

a visitor playing with *Tactophonics* through a tree branch

Andrew Cook meets communication aids

keyguard on a Toby Churchill Lightwriter communication aid

communication aids

In the chapter **expression meets information**, I argued that our interactions with communication aids are being inappropriately dictated by the technology inside them. Products containing a computer need not be conceived of as computers; what is happening *below the waterline* need not be visible above. And while text-to-speech technology will continue to underpin synthesized speech, this doesn't mean that our interactions with it have to stop at typing text. Being limited to text is limiting how expressive an AAC user can be.

Interaction designers could and should play more of a role. Of course, the most important aspect of the interaction design of AAC devices is not a person's interaction with the device itself but rather her interactions with her conversational partners. How could communication aids support this in more ways than they currently are?

Andrew Cook

Andrew Cook is a young interaction designer and computer musician (under the name Samoyed). These two fields came together in his design of *Tactophonics*, a kit that allows musicians to physically manipulate computer-generated sounds. "Sitting at a laptop, using keyboard and trackpad, you are just making choices," he says, "controlling the sound but not really manipulating it. I was trying to move the computer musician's role away from that of a *process manager* and back to being a *performer*."[1]

Cook is a recent graduate in Interactive Media Design at the University of Dundee, a program run by both the School of Computing (which has a deep experience of assistive technology) and the School of Design (which like most art schools doesn't, but provides a complementary background). Interdisciplinary design education can challenge the artificial division between art and science that lies behind many of the tensions in this book. Cook had the technical skills to build

Mast gives a performance of computer music

working prototypes, wire up contact microphones, and write sound-processing code, but always in order to explore, rather than letting this become a technological end in itself. His work is often playful, but thoughtful and with serious intent.

meeting

There are definitely similarities between some of the issues facing computer music and those in AAC, each arising from rather old-fashioned views of how we should interact with computers. A person using a communication aid is also restricted to making selections—selecting words and basic intonation via punctuation. In AAC, though, user interfaces are frequently built to be accessed through a single switch or a switch array instead of even a keyboard, in order to accommodate a wide range of physical impairment that may accompany speech impairment. These additional restrictions take the role of the user even further toward Cook's notion of a process manager.

performance and practice

As recording artists, computer musicians now have access to more freedom than ever before. Yet as performers, they may struggle to connect with an audience. Music performed directly from laptop computers can be a deeply dissatisfying experience for an audience, since listeners cannot tell what sounds are prestored, which are being manipulated in some way during the performance, and which are being instigated live. As a computer musician himself, Cook was equally inspired by his frustration as a performer: "Giving a performance can be an unrewarding experience because it is so difficult to establish a rapport with an audience, so difficult to get a reaction at the time."[2] The most spontaneous improvisation may be misread as a skillfully crafted prerecording.

Communication aids less obviously suffer from the same issues of unreadability. It may not be clear to a conversational

Andrew Cook's *Tactophonics* kit, allowing interaction with computer
music through found objects

partner what control people have over their AAC device's tone of voice, and there is a danger in this ambiguity either way: if it is assumed that the user is in control of the fine nuances of intonation (which current devices do not allow) and this intonation is inappropriate, then the user may be held socially inept; whereas if the other person's perception is that there is no control, that the technology is determining intonation on the user's behalf, then it might be assumed that the user is not capable of deciding, perhaps that they are emotionally impaired. So there is not only an issue of controlling tone of voice but also of being *seen* to be in control of the tone of voice.

Cook designed *Tactophonics* to make a musician's actions legible, even theatrical. Instead of playing a laptop directly, *Tactophonics* allows a performer to play pretty much any object they wish; contact microphones on the object respond to its physical manipulation, not producing sound directly, but generating parameters by which synthesized sounds are shaped. *Tactophonics* is in the form of a beautifully designed toolkit that lets performers choose an object that enriches their onstage act. Cook says he was surprised by just how imaginative people's choices have been: musicians have chosen the branch of a tree, a baseball bat, and a full set of crockery.

A more expressive communication device would take more practice to use skillfully. The words *performance* versus *use* imply very different demands and expectations. What if a communication aid sounded different if the keys were punched than if they were pressed, if manual nuance were translated into vocal nuance? How much practice would be appropriate to master this? Would it be unethical to design more expressive communication devices that demanded good motor control, given that speech impairment is often associated with other physical impairments? Or might more expressive but more demanding interfaces in turn inspire new approaches for people without fine motor control?

Trimpin's *Klompen*, an installation of 120 wooden clogs with computer-controlled solenoids

primitive instruments and prepared pianos

If we do try to introduce more of an element of expression and performance into communication devices, a real danger is in knowing where to draw the line. The complexity of speech—in which voice quality, pitch, amplitude, intonation, aspiration, accent, nasality, and so many other variables contribute—far exceeds the range of sounds of any musical instrument. Attempting to control more than a fraction of this at any one time can lead to the kind of research prototype that requires the coordination of a young fighter pilot. Whereas it might be interesting to develop simple prototypes that nonetheless benefited from the ear of a concert violinist.

Cook thinks that primitive instruments offer a better starting point. We can approach even as surreal an instrument as a tree branch with an instinct for how we might interact with it, and a broad idea of how it might sound. "Although it's not until you start playing it, hearing back the results of your actions," explains Cook, "that you really start to understand it."[3]

Even if direct, physical manipulation is not appropriate because of dexterity impairment, materials can still be used expressively. A *prepared piano* has had its sound altered by placing objects on or between its strings, hammers, or dampers. This introduces another phase of expressiveness, somewhere between practice and performance, between composition and improvisation: that of preparing the instrument itself. The ability to do this in one's own time, at one's own pace, might make this an appropriate model for AAC users.

AAC devices are customized to their user's requirements with the help of language and occupational therapists. To a designer, the words *user*, *customize*, and *device* have rather functional connotations. A *performer* *experimenting* and creating his own *instrument* implies a different relationship between that person and the technology, that person and the design team.

dark chocolate and rich fruitcake

The common ground between primitive instruments and prepared pianos is materiality—in this case, the acoustic qualities of materials. Materials play a role in our experience of sound whether or not we are touching them or producing the sounds ourselves. Cook is inspired by the artist Trimpin, whose sound sculptures combine the acoustic and iconic properties of materials. In Trimpin's *Klompen*, 120 wooden clogs are suspended from the ceiling by wires that connect them to a computer. As the computer coordinates the triggering of solenoid-driven hammers in each clog, a percussive rhythm resonates around the gallery and the clogs also *dance* in the air.

Cook is intrigued by the idea of introducing materiality into AAC, using materials to select and manipulate tone of voice. People have enormous sensitivity to vocal nuance, but may have difficulty describing this directly; perhaps materials can be used to translate. This reminds me of a training session when I started as a lecturer in which a voice coach complimented me on a hint of *dark chocolate* in my voice to imply a low pitch, a richness, even a fluid intonation. This is a pretty abstract allusion, but somehow I was able to imagine the sound qualities he was referring to.

What voice qualities might other materials represent? Our first, obvious ideas seem disappointing—of sandpaper being used to describe a harsh or rasping voice, or glass being used to portray a clear yet cutting one. Then Cook remembers a voice being described as a *rich fruitcake*, an allusion that seems to go further still than chocolate, suggesting accent and vocabulary, and the possibilities start to expand. And when combined with action, they expand still further.

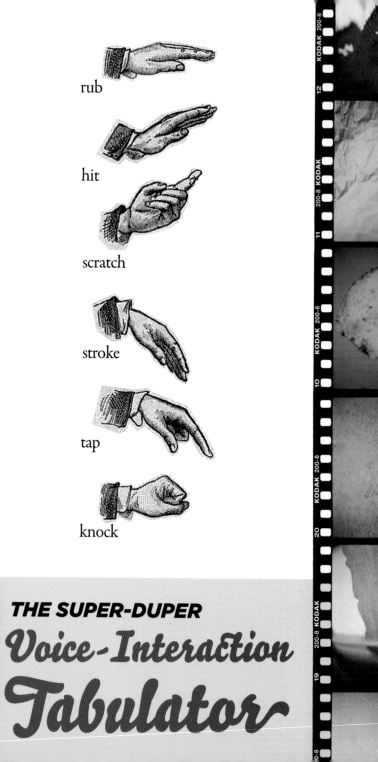

rub

hit

scratch

stroke

tap

knock

THE SUPER-DUPER
Voice-Interaction
Tabulator

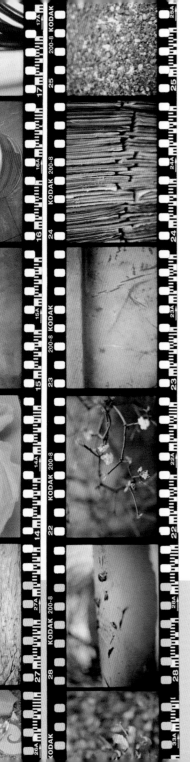

fervently
hesitantly
softly
angrily
languidly
playfully
furiously

INSTRUCTIONS

Choose 1 item from each column: 1 **action**,
1 **material** and 1 **descriptor.** eg. *stroke + blossom + languidly; scratch + bark + hesitantly*

How would that sound as a description of
voice quality? Put on the voice. Go on! **Do
the voice!**

Teddy Blood Bag Radio by Dunne & Raby in the Energy Gallery of the Science Museum, London

if Dunne & Raby met memory aids

If design has done less to engage with some disabilities than others—less with sensory impairment than mobility impairment, for example—then an area it has made little contribution to at all is cognitive impairment. Perhaps one reason cognitive impairment is difficult for any design team is that it is so difficult to imagine what it must be like. While product development teams may employ clouded glasses and stiffened gloves that simulate visual and dexterity impairment, and thus offer some small insight into how profound these can be, empathizing with someone with cognitive impairment is so much harder, if not impossible, for someone without even secondhand experience. But the very intangibility of cognitive impairment may also point to contributions that design could make.

giving invisible issues visibility

Dunne & Raby are pioneers of the approach of *critical design*: design that does not seek to provide solutions to often complex and sensitive issues but instead aims to ask questions and catalyze discussion. An inherent part of provoking dialogue is to make hidden issues visible and tangible, whether through furniture that reacts to invisible electromagnetic radiation or objects giving iconic presence to the domestic implications of future energy policies. What issues around disability remain un- or underdiscussed? How might design render them more visible, even deliberately more controversial or confrontational? How else could design help?

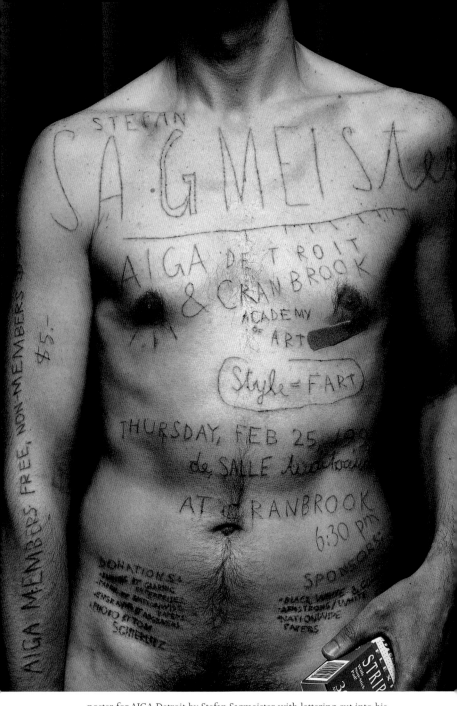

poster for AIGA Detroit by Stefan Sagmeister with lettering cut into his skin by Martin Woodtli

if Stefan Sagmeister met accessibility signage

Disability is represented internationally by a pictogram likely to perpetuate the stereotype of a disabled person as an adult male wheelchair user. Ambiguously, this icon is sometimes used to indicate wheelchair access and sometimes to denote generic accessibility. Icons for other impairments, such as ears and eyes with lines through them, do little to illuminate the diversity of even less visible disabilities. More radical approaches are needed as well. Stefan Sagmeister is a graphic designer whose iconoclasm could open up new ways of thinking. His most provocative work, featured in the appropriately named book *Made You Look*, includes a poster for the AIGA infamously cut into his own skin.[1]

avoiding a predictable response

Sometimes appropriately shocking and sometimes deliberately understated, Sagmeister frequently steps back from a predictable response. An annual report that he designed for the Zumtobel lighting company has an enigmatic plain white molded cover. Inside, the book is divided by photographs of this molding lit in different ways, throwing the form into different colors and relief; the design comes from the lighting itself. These days he devotes a quarter of his energies to "socially responsible design" projects, working with people whose aims he admires, where "their goal could be achieved faster with good design." But he resists the urge to represent social or political campaigns with trite logos, or "cheesy ideas like drawings of people holding hands."[2] Disability demands and deserves more diverse and more sophisticated approaches.

Vexed SABS coat provides freedom of movement despite apparent
constriction

Vexed meets wheelchair capes

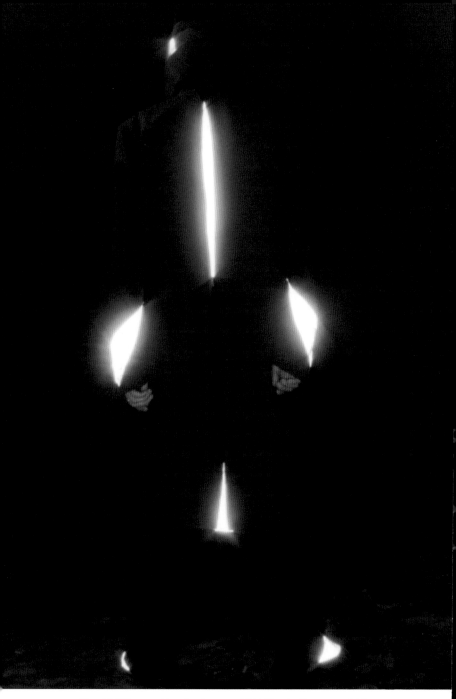

Vexed SABS coat with reflective material hidden inside vents, which open up when the wearer bends forward over bicycle handlebars

wheelchair capes

It can be difficult keeping dry in the rain while sitting down, as anyone who has ridden a bicycle, used a wheelchair, or sat on a bench during a storm knows. Water will run down and collect in the sitter's lap, or between them and the seat, and find its way between layers of clothing and through even water-resistant fabrics. Designing truly waterproof but wearable clothing for any of these activities is a demanding task.

Protection from the weather in a wheelchair is particularly challenging, since reduced mobility will prevent most wheelchair users from standing up and balancing on one leg while pulling on or off another layer of clothing. This has led to the persistence of capes for wheelchairs, whereas capes have gone out of fashion for cycling—my father (who in his own time built joystick keyboards for disabled children, my first awareness of this field) used to have one in the 1950s, and he wore it unselfconsciously with khaki Scout shorts. Furthermore, a wheelchair cape for someone who propels her own manual wheelchair has to allow arm movement for reaching backward and forward. These criteria tend to lead to capes that are voluminous.

Add a hood, and the result can have the look of a shapeless anorak, practical and pragmatic, but hardly fashionable. If there could be said to be an aesthetic at all, it is inherited from rural outdoor pursuits, rambling, or hiking. Yet these may not be the most appropriate associations in an urban context, especially among young people wanting the respect of their peers within an urban street culture.

Vexed

Fashion company Vexed Design would be well-placed to reconcile these agendas, having brought an edgy, urban perspective to highly practical and technical clothing. Its coats are made from waterproof and even knife-proof fabrics. Vexed's SABS coat has vents that open as the wearer leans forward to

hood of Ninja jacket by Vexed Generation

hold bicycle handlebars to reveal flashes of reflective material, providing visibility when cycling at night that can go unseen when walking around during the day.

In its *Bespoke* collection for Transport for London, Vexed has created clothing that offers "cycling utility without being defined by a cycling aesthetic."[1] Urban commuters may cycle five kilometers to work and back, but spend the majority of their day off their bike without wishing to look like cycle couriers. *Bespoke* is designed for both on and off the bike.

Vexed Generation was founded in 1992 by Adam Thorpe and Joe Hunter, neither of whom had a formal fashion training. "We weren't told how to do anything," says Thorpe. "And we like to keep ourselves a bit ignorant," adds Hunter.[2] Over the past seventeen years, they say that they have grown better at their trade, turning to tailors they know for advice, but using this resource sparingly. An acquired knowledge of the "finer engineered details of welt pockets" combined with a deliberate naivety has allowed them to question received wisdom, often working with manufacturers to reinvent traditional fabrics as technical materials such as reflective tweed and Teflon-treated denim.[3]

The Ninja fleece was adopted by British snowboarders on the ski slopes as much as by people in the cities. This underlines the sophistication of the materials and construction, but Thorpe thinks that the real reason snowboarders appropriated it was that the Ninja offered a black alternative to the garish colors of snowboarding fashion at the time. "The 'street' was Los Angeles, not our street."[4] Vexed Generation was linked to the world around it, inspired by moving around London's streets as well as designing for its experience of raves, marches, and cold, wet days.

the Vexed Parka, an ambiguous meeting of self-protection, privacy, and
political subversion

meeting

This leads Hunter to a first train of thought: how to design a wheelchair cape so that it becomes a "must-have" garment even if one isn't a wheelchair user. Thorpe calls this "designing in appropriation."[5] A combination of practicality and urbanity could obviously bring fresh and refreshing perspectives to wheelchair clothing.

Vexed has also explored the topology of clothing, through garments that look constraining yet allow full body movement. Inspired by Dior's *La Normandie*—a jacket without sleeves or armholes so the wearer was rendered incapable of anything other than standing as a pillar of elegance, and needed assistance to drink a cocktail or smoke a cigarette—Vexed's *Wrap Liberation* appears to be restrictive but is in fact quite practical. So wheelchair garments that allow movement need not look ill fitting; they could even deliberately look confining.

political design

Vexed clothing also has a political dimension. When they founded the company, Thorpe and Hunter were inspired to create clothing not only beneficial to the idea of urban mobility but also relevant to its darker side: air pollution, constant surveillance, and curtailed civil liberties. The Vexed Parka conceals the wearer's face, but it is not clear whether this is to afford protection from traffic pollution or surveillance cameras. And it has ballistic nylon reinforcement at the neck and crutch to protect against common police arrest maneuvers. Do these capabilities make the wearer more secure, or more deserving of suspicion?

In the early days of Vexed, many customers were attracted to the idea of Vexed garments as a manifesto, as "flyers you can wear."[6] These days Vexed is comfortable saying that its clothes are trying to be more attractive, and describes its work as "more sympathetic."[7] Nevertheless, how might Vexed reinvent the wheelchair cape—practically, fashionably, provocatively, and politically?

wet mobility, wheeled mobility

As we start talking about wheelchair capes, the conversation alternates between these political issues and technical details. In the past Vexed has taken the vents in a riding coat that open up to let it drape over the back of the horse and applied these to the foreleg of a coat for cyclists, allowing movement for pedaling. I am unable to follow a discussion between Thorpe and Hunter about stretch panels, run-off gutters, and thermal regulation. Then we're speaking about canoes; perhaps if part of the waterproof cape were a skirt, built into and seen as being part of the wheelchair, the wearer could put on a shorter, more conventional jacket that could be zipped into this?

When they talk through any brief, sometimes the direction will be articulated in words and sometimes it will come out of the details. They are skeptical of some conceptual industrial design, which has the danger of just being "pub talk with illustrations," and would not want to approach a brief of this nature without an understanding of the engineering involved, including engineers as well as wheelchair users, but also spending a rainy week in a wheelchair themselves.[8]

the urban mobility cape

Thorpe and Hunter wonder whether it would be possible to design an urban mobility cape, a garment that would have an appeal across cyclists, wheelchair users, and scooter riders. This brings together design for the object with design for the person, requiring a deep understanding of the technicalities of bicycles, wheelchairs, and scooters, but also the sensibilities of who is being designed for. These sensibilities would for once not be defined by ability, perhaps not even by age group, but by some other, more complex measure of culture.

wheelchair capes inspire Vexed

I am struck by how many of the themes of this book recur in this one conversation. We are definitely in the territory between *fashion* and *discretion*, although in Vexed's case this has often involved creating garments that are at once more fashionable and more discreet in an urban setting. *Exploring* and *solving* are both at the heart of Vexed's approach, inspired by a political vision and informed by technical details, which together lead to more diversity than the market convergence on a sports aesthetic. *Identity* and *ability* are inherent in the idea that a wheelchair user might want to be defined by an urban street culture, not by wheelchair use—and the urban mobility cape is a clear example of *resonant design*. *Provocation* and *sensitivity* are contained in the political but responsive grounding of all of Vexed's work.

They may not yet have designed specifically for disability, but Thorpe thinks "our clothes are assistive technology."[9] They are conscious of the need to learn more from disabled people, yet their years of experience makes them, like many other designers, experts in many of the issues that could redefine design against disability. Most of all, talking about wheelchair capes Vexed is passionate yet down-to-earth, challenging yet respectful. Once more *disability inspires design*. "Ask a different question and you get a different answer," says Hunter.[10] This is true for both cultures: just as disability could inspire fashion design, so urban culture could inspire design for disability.

overleaf: Vexed get inspired by issues and details for the urban mobility cape

ORGANIZE ALL CHAIR COMPONENTS

//TRAIN DRAIN TO HOLES

DO WE NEED TO KEEP THE CHAIR DRY? OR JUST THE PERSON?

ALL WATER RUNS OFF

TEFLON COAT CHAIR
CLIMATE CONTROL →
WATER PROOF
WEARER

DRAINAGE HOLES IN SEAT → NO PUDDLES IN CHAIR

UNIVERSALITY - fit/function on ALL? types of chair?

CROSS-BACK-STRETCH
ABRASION RESISTANCE UNDER-ARM

Panel/S... Sittin... Po...

Accessories
Solution divided between several separate products - Modular
DUALITY
Fashion + Function
Glove outer   aesthetic Functional
Glove inner   durable

Back of the Upper & Lower Arm
Shoulder Blades & Spine
Hand, Wrist & Elbow
Coccyx (Tailbone & Hips)
Feet, especially the Heels and Toes

Redneck...

SOLUTION

HYDROPHOBIC
CHAIR → ALL CHAIR COMPONENTS PLASMARIZED? } CHAIR IS...
         → DRAINAGE IN CHAIR SEAT/perforation
NOW ⟹ ONLY HAVE TO DEAL WITH DRESSING THE PERS...
→ NO HOOD → WEAR ANY HAT YOU WANT/OR NOT!   ° Ru...
BIG ISSUE: LAP WATER MANAGEMENT -----

Ste...
Sho...

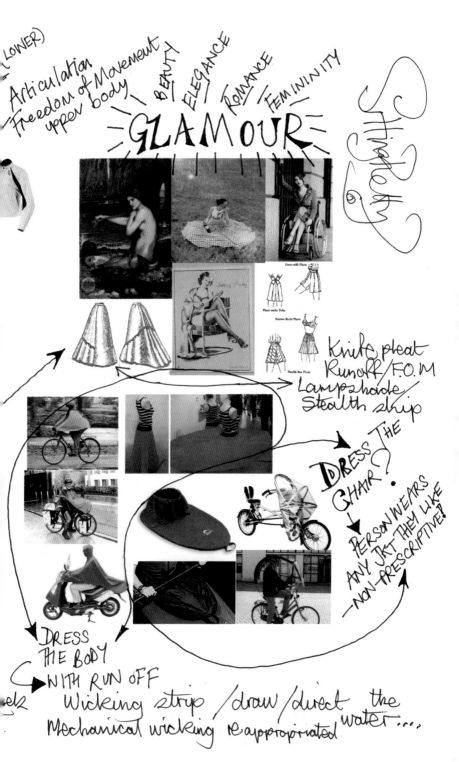

(LOWER)

Articulation
Freedom of Movement
upper body
BEAUTY ELEGANCE ROMANCE FEMININITY

GLAMOUR

High(ER)

Knife pleat
Runoff/F.O.M
Lampshade/
Stealth ship

DRESS THE
CHAIR?

PERSON WEARS
ANY JKT THEY LIKE
—NON-PRESCRIPTIVE?

DRESS
THE BODY
WITH RUN OFF
Wicking strip /draw /direct the
Mechanical wicking reappropriated water....

conclusion

Love Letters eyewear by Cutler and Gross, designed by Monica Chong with words written by Napoléon Bonaparte to Joséphine

creative tensions

The main chapters of this book have challenged some of the traditional priorities of design for disability. Yet challenging the absolute priority of discretion does not imply dismissing its importance altogether, just acknowledging its relationship to other issues, currently all but absent in design for disability, although alive within fashion design. Both fashion *and* discretion are necessary influences, as are exploring and solving, simplicity and universality, provoking and respecting, feeling and testing, expression and meaning. Like antagonistic pairs of muscles, opposing biceps and triceps, these conflicting priorities might seem to work against each other, but together they afford control of force, position, and direction.

The design issues around disability are underexplored, and demand and deserve far more radical approaches, whereas art school iconoclasm is conspicuous by its absence. What is needed is truly interdisciplinary design thinking, combining and blurring design craft with engineering brilliance, therapeutic excellence, and the broadest experiences of disabled people.

This additional complexity of issues, people, and cultures will initially make things even more difficult. Some of the old certainties of design for disability will need to be reconsidered. Absolute, sometimes quantifiable priorities will have to be replaced by more elusive balances. The inherent tensions will lead to heated debate—at times a seeming drain on resources as well as a source of positive energy. But these tensions do need to be embraced. Anything less is a recipe for mediocrity, and mediocrity would be more insulting than controversy.

beyond traditional views of function

In a rare interview with the Design Museum, Jonathan Ive was asked what distinguished the products that his team at Apple develops. "Perhaps the decisive factor is fanatical care beyond the obvious stuff: the obsessive attention to details

Apple iPod shuffle designed by Jonathan Ive's industrial design group

that are often overlooked," he answered. The best design may appear obvious in hindsight and may belie the effort that went into it, in Ive's words "genuinely taking the time, investing the resources and caring enough to try and make something better."[1]

As an industrial design student at Newcastle Polytechnic, Ive chose a hearing aid as his major project. He was drawn to a special category of products that to their wearers were more an imperative than a consumer choice, yet despite this importance seemed to be designed to fulfill a functional requirement, with little care going into anything else. Ive still talks of "caring beyond the functional imperative, we also acknowledge that products have a significance way beyond traditional views of function."[2]

This echoes the words of Charles Eames in an interview in 1968 on the subject "What Is Design?" The interviewer asked whether design implies "the idea of products that are necessarily useful," rather than "solely for pleasure." Eames's reply challenged this distinction: "Who would say that pleasure is not useful?"[3]

designers meet disabilities

The role of this book is catalytic, to inspire wider and deeper examples of collaboration between individual designers, development teams, and disabled people than are contained within its pages. The complex relationships between these issues will be best played out within close working relationships.

I hope that these collaborations are not restricted to the obvious pairings but that businesses, institutes, teams, and individuals will have the vision to seek out more imaginative partnerships—with design disciplines not directly related to the industry, and with the enfants terribles as well as the safe pairs of hands. The risks of such meetings may be high, but the potential rewards are even higher. Design for disability might yet be turned on its head by the combined influences of

Charles and Ray Eames's DCW chair, inspired by their leg splint

Chalayan, Sagmeister, Ive, Dunne & Raby, and others, in the way that so many other fields of design have been revolutionized.

design inspires design

I hope that the ideas contained in this book will come to be better represented by examples than in writing. The many different ways of resolving these tensions will be best communicated through exemplars, better represented by practice than by theory, once design meets disability.

In return, design constantly absorbs influences and mutates them in doing so, is reinvented not just by new information but also by new juxtapositions of people, material, media, and ideas. Charles and Ray Eames's plywood furniture not only evolved from their leg splint but was inspired by it too. Ive's ceramic-like hearing aid led to a commission for Ideal Standard that set his career in motion. Design inspires design. When design meets disability, this meeting will change design itself.

notes

when the Eameses met leg splints

1. Madame L'Amic of the Musée des Arts Décoratifs in Paris, interviewing Charles Eames for the exhibition catalog for "What Is Design?" (1968), reprinted in John Neuhart, Marilyn Neuhart, and Ray Eames, *Eames Design: The Work of the Office of Charles and Ray Eames* (New York: Harry N. Abrams Inc., 1989).

introduction

1. World Health Organization, *International Classification of Functioning, Disability, and Health* (fifty-fourth World Health Assembly, ninth plenary meeting, May 22, 2001).

2. RNIB website (http://www.rnib.org.uk); RNID website (http://www.rnid.org.uk).

3. Department for Children, Schools, and Families website (http://www.dfes.gov.uk); Learning Disabilities Association of America website (http://www.ldanatl.org).

4. Design Against Crime website (http://www.designagainstcrime.org).

fashion meets discretion

1. Joanna Lewis, "Vision for Britain: the NHS, the Optical Industry, and Spectacle Design, 1946–1986" (MA dissertation, Royal College of Art, 2001).

2. Ibid., quoted in Lucy Zimmermann, Michael Hillman, and John Clarkson, "Wheelchairs: From Engineering to Inclusive Design" (paper presented at Include, the International Conference on Inclusive Design, Royal College of Art, London, April 5–8, 2005).

3. Ibid.

4. Akiko Busch, "From Stigma to Status: The Specification of Spectacles," *Metropolis* 10, no. 8 (April 1991): 35–37, quoted in Zimmerman, Hillman, and Clarkson, "Wheelchairs."

5. Ibid.

6. Alain Mikli website (http://www.mikli.com).

7. Per Mollerup, *Collapsible* (San Francisco: Chronicle Books, 2001).

8. Cutler and Gross website (http://www.cutlerandgross.co.uk).

9. Henrietta Thompson, "Listen Up: HearWear Is Here," *Blueprint*, no. 232 (July 2005).

10. Alexander McQueen, "Fashion-able?" *Dazed & Confused*, no. 46 (September 1998).

11. Aimee Mullins, personal communication, January 10, 2008.

12. Ibid.

13. Ibid.

14. Ibid.

15. Ibid.

16. H2.0 symposium archive website (<http://h20.media.mit.edu).

17. Jacques Monestier, quoted by E. Jane Dickson in *Golden Touch* (magazine cutting in author's possession from around 1993). See also Jacques Monestier's website "Automata Maker and Sculptor" (http://www.jacques-monestier.com).

exploring meets solving

1. Lucy Zimmermann, Michael Hillman, and John Clarkson, "Wheelchairs: From Engineering to Inclusive Design" (paper presented at Include, the International Conference on Inclusive Design, Royal College of Art, London, April 5–8, 2005).

2. Brian Woods and Nick Watson, "A Glimpse at the Social and Technological History of Wheelchairs," *International Journal of Therapy and Rehabilitation* 11, no. 9 (2004): 407–410.

3. Marisa Bartolucci, "By Design: Making a Chair Able," *Metropolis* 12, no. 4 (November 1992): 29–33.

4. Alan Newell, "Inclusive Design or Assistive Technology," in *Inclusive Design: Design for the Whole Population*, ed. John Clarkson, Roger Coleman, Simeon Keates, and Cherie Lebbon (London: Springer, 2003), 172–181.

5. Johan Barber, "The Design of Disability Products: A Psychological Perspective," *British Journal of Occupational Therapy* 59, no. 12 (1996): 561–564.

6. Charlotte Fiell and Peter Fiell, *1000 Chairs* (Cologne: Taschen, 2000); Charlotte Fiell and Peter Fiell, *1000 Lights* (Cologne: Taschen, 2006).

7. Forgotten Chairs website (http://imd.dundee.ac.uk/forgottenchairs); see also the original Museum of Lost Interactions website (http://imd.dundee.ac.uk/moli).

8. Nextmaruni website (http://www.nextmaruni.com).

9. Ibid.

10. Motivation website (http://www.motivation.org).

11. David Constantine, Catherine Hingley, and Jennifer Howitt, "Donated Wheelchairs in Low-Income Countries: Issues and Alternative Methods for Improving Wheelchair Provision" (paper presented at the Fourth International Seminar on Appropriate Healthcare Technologies for Developing Countries, Institution of Electrical Engineers [became Institution of Engineering and Technology], London, May 23–24, 2006).

12. Lisa White, ed., "Blind Design" special issue, *InteriorView*, no. 14 (June 1999).

13. Bodo Sperlein, personal communication, November 16, 2007. See also Bodo Sperlein's website (http://www.bodosperlein.com).

14. Ibid.

15. David Werner, *Nothing about Us without Us: Developing Innovative Technologies for, by, and with Disabled Persons* (Palo Alto, CA: HealthWrights, 1998).

simple meets universal

1. John Clarkson, Roger Coleman, Simeon Keates, and Cherie Lebbon, eds., *Inclusive Design: Design for the Whole Population* (London: Springer, 2003)

2. Apple Inc., "100 Million iPods Sold," press release, April 9, 2007, on Apple Inc. website (http://www.apple.com/pr/library/2007/04/09ipod.html).

3. Blaise Pascal, "Je n'ai fait celle-ci plus longue que parceque je n'ai pas eu le loisir de la faire plus courte," in *Provincial Letters*, letter 16, December 4, 1656, reprinted in Blaise Pascal, *The Provincial Letters* (Eugene, OR: Wipf & Stock Publishers, 1997).

4. Apple Inc., "Apple Presents iPod: Ultra-Portable MP3 Music Player Puts 1,000 Songs in Your Pocket," press release, October 23, 2001, on Apple Inc. website (http://www.apple.com/pr/library/2001/oct/23ipod.html).

5. Quoted by Leander Kahney in "Straight Dope on the iPod's Birth," *Wired News*, October 17, 2006, on Wired website (http://www.wired.com/gadgets/mac/commentary/cultofmac/2006/10/71956).

6. Bruce Sterling, *Shaping Things* (Cambridge, MA: MIT Press, 2006).

7. Ibid.

8. Ibid.

9. Fiona MacCarthy, "House Style," *Guardian*, November 17, 2007. See also *Guardian* website (http://books.guardian.co.uk/review/story/0,,2212244,00.html).

10. Christopher Frayling, interviewed on "Desert Island Discs," BBC Radio 4, November 2, 2003.

11. Michael Evamy, "Able Bodies," *Design* (Spring 1997): 20–25.

12. Ibid., 5.

13. Quoted by Erika Germer, "Steve Jobs," *Fast Company* (October 1999). See also Fast Company website (http://www.fastcompany.com/articles/1999/11/steve_jobs.html)

14. John Maeda, *Simplicity* (Cambridge, MA: MIT Press, 2006).

identity meets ability

1. World Health Organization, *International Classification of Functioning, Disability, and Health*, (fifty-fourth world health assembly, ninth plenary meeting, May 22, 2001). See also ICF website (http://www.who.int/classifications/icf/site/icftemplate.cfm).

2. Ibid.

3. Ibid.

4. Alan Newell and Peter Gregor, "Human-Computer Interfaces for People with Disabilities," in *Handbook of Human-Computer Interaction*, ed. Martin Helander, Thomas Landauer, and Prasad Prabhu (Amsterdam: Elsevier Science Publishing, 1997), 813–824.

5. Ibid., 1.

6. Ibid.

7. Jeremy Myerson, *IDEO: Masters of Innovation* (London: Laurence King, 2004).

8. Ibid., 4.

9. Sebastien Sablé and Dominique Archambault, "BlindStation: A Game Platform Adapted to Visually Impaired Children" (paper presented at the Cambridge Workshop on Universal Access and Assistive Technology, Trinity Hall, Cambridge, March 25–27, 2001); also in *Universal Access and Assistive Technology*, ed. Simeon Keates, Patrick Langdon, John Clarkson, and Peter Robinson (London: Springer-Verlag, 2002).

10. Steve Tyler, personal communication, January 17, 2005.

11. Tissot, *Silen-T User's Manual*, available online on Tissot website (http://www.tissot.ch).

12. Crispin Jones, *Mr Jones Watches*, 2004. See also Crispin Jones's website (http://www.mr-jones.org).

13. Fondation de la haute horlogerie website (http://www.hautehorlogerie.org/en/encyclopaedia/glossary/tact-watch-1585.html).

14. Tanya Weaver, "Hear and Now," *New Design* 36 (December 2005): 34–39.

provocative meets sensitive

1. Charlotte Higgins, "Quinn Prepares to Unveil Trafalgar Square Sculpture," *Guardian*, September 13, 2005. See also *Guardian* website (http://www.guardian.co.uk/uk/2005/sep/13/arts.artsnews).

2. Alison Lapper's website (http://www.alisonlapper.com).

3. Rachel Cooke, "Bold, Brave, Beautiful," *Observer*, September 18, 2005.

4. Ibid.

5. Ibid., 2.

6. Alison Lapper and Guy Feldman, *My Life in My Hands* (New York: Simon and Schuster, 2005).

7. Dawn Ades, Linda Theophilus, Clare Doherty et al., *Cosy: Freddie Robins* (Colchester: Firstsite Publishers, 2002).

8. Mark Prest, curator, "Adorn, Equip," City Gallery, Leicester and touring exhibition, 2001. See also Adorn, Equip website (http://www.adornequip.co.uk).

9. Anthony Dunne and Fiona Raby, *Design Noir: The Secret Life of Electronic Objects* (Basel: Birkhäuser, 2001); Anthony Dunne, *Hertzian Tales: Electronic Products, Aesthetic Experience, and Critical Design*, rev. ed. (Cambridge, MA: MIT Press, 2006.

10. Ibid.

11. Kelly Dobson, personal communication, December 16, 2004.

12. Kelly Dobson, "Wearable Body Organs: Critical Cognition Becomes (Again) Somatic," in *Proceedings of the 5th Conference on Creativity and Cognition* (New York: Association for Computing Machinery, 2005), 259–262.

13. Clare Hocking, "Function or Feelings: Factors in Abandonment of Assistive Devices," *Technology and Disability* 11, nos. 1–2 (1999): 3–11.

14. MA Design Interactions website (http://www.rca.ac.uk/pages/study/ma_interaction_design_171.html).

15. Marcus Fairs, *Twenty-first Century Design* (London: Carlton Books, 2006).

16. Crispin Jones, Graham Pullin, Mat Hunter, Anton Schubert, Paul South, Lynda Patrick, Andrew Hirniak et al., *Social Mobiles* (London: IDEO, 2005).

17. Tom Standage, "Think Before You Talk: Can Technology Make Mobile Phones Less Socially Disruptive?" *Economist*, January 18, 2003.

18. BlindKiss website (http://www.blindkiss.com).

19. Ibid.

feeling meets testing

1. Simeon Keates, Patrick Langdon, John Clarkson, and Peter Robinson, eds., *Universal Access and Assistive Technology* (London: Springer-Verlag, 2002).

2. Jeremy Myerson, *IDEO: Masters of Innovation* (London: Laurence King, 2001).

3. Duncan Kerr, personal communication, 1997.

4. Marion Buchenau and Jane Fulton Suri, "Experience Prototyping," in *Proceedings of the 3rd Conference on Designing Interactive Systems: Processes, Practices, Methods, and Techniques* (New York: Association for Computing Machinery, 2000), pp. 424–433.

5. Ibid.

6. See also Graham Pullin and Martin Bontoft, "Connecting Business, Inclusion, and Design," in *Inclusive Design: Designing for the Whole Population*, ed. John Clarkson, Roger Coleman, Simeon Keates, and Cherie Lebbon (London: Springer, 2003), pp. 206–214 .

7. Roger Orpwood, personal communication, November 10, 2006

8. Roger Orpwood, Chris Gibbs, et al., "The Design of Smart Homes for People with Dementia: User Interface Aspects," *Universal Access in the Information Society* 4, no. 2 (December 2005).

9. Ibid., 7.

10. Ibid.

11. Helen Petrie, Fraser Hamilton, et al., "Remote Usability Evaluations with Disabled People," *Proceedings of the SIGCHI Conference on Human Factors in Computing Systems* (2006) (New York: Association for Computing Machinery, 2006).

12. Jacob Beaver, Andy Boucher, and Sarah Pennington, eds., *The Curious Home* (London: Interaction Research Studio, Goldsmiths College, 2007).

13. Bill Gaver, John Bowers, et al., "The Drift Table: Designing for Ludic Engagement," *Proceedings of CHI* (2004) (New York: Association for Computing Machinery, 2004).

14. Anthony Dunne and Fiona Raby, "The *Placebo* Project," in *Proceedings of Designing Interactive Systems* (2002) (New York: Association for Computing Machinery, 2002).

15. Lauren Parker quoted in Anthony Dunne and Fiona Raby, *Design Noir: The Secret Life of Electronic Objects* (Basel: Birkhäuser, 2001).

expression meets information

1. David Crystal, *The Cambridge Encyclopaedia of the English Language* (Cambridge: Cambridge University Press, 1995).

2. John Holmes and Wendy Holmes, *Speech Synthesis and Recognition*, 2nd ed. (London: Taylor and Francis, 2001).

3. Alan Newell, "Today's Dreams, Tomorrow's Reality" (Phonic Ear Distinguished Lecture), *Augmentative and Alternative Communication*, June 8, 1992, 1–8.

4. Bill Moggridge, *Designing Interactions* (Cambridge, MA: MIT Press, 2006).

5. Graham Pullin and Norman Alm, "The Speaking Mobile: Provoking New Approaches to AAC Design" (paper presented at the International Conference on Augmentative and Alternative Communication, Düsseldorf, Germany, August 2006).

6. Traveleyes website (http://www.traveleyes.co.uk).

7. Wolfgang von Kempelen, *Mechanismus der menschlichen Sprache nebst Beschreibung einer sprechenden Maschine* (Vienna: J. B. Degen, 1791).

8. Annalu Waller, personal communication, September 9, 2005.

9. Norman Alm and Alan Newell, "Being an Interesting Conversation Partner," in *Augmentative and Alternative Communication: European Perspectives*, ed. Stephen von Tetzchner and Mogens Jensen (London: Whurr Publishers, 1996).

10. Erik Blankinship and Richard Beckwith, "Tools for Expressive Text-to-Speech Markup" (paper presented at the Fourteenth Annual

Association of Computing Machinery Symposium on User Interface Software and Technology, Orlando, Florida, 2001).

11. Stephen Hawking's website (http://www.hawking.org.uk/disable/dindex.htm).

12. Ibid.

13. Laurie Anderson, quoted, among other places, on University of Chicago website (http://www.ucls.uchicago.edu/about/message/1007.shtml).

14. Mark Hansen and Ben Rubin, "Listening Post: Giving Voice to Online Communication," in *Proceedings of the 2002 International Conference on Auditory Display* (New York: Association of Computing Machinery, 2002).

15. Marion Buchenau and Jane Fulton Suri, "Experience Prototyping," in *Proceedings of the 3rd Conference on Designing Interactive Systems: Processes, Practices, Methods, and Techniques* (New York: Association for Computing Machinery, 2000), pp. 424–433.

16. Urtica website (http://www.urtica.org).

17. Abraham Moles, *Information Theory and Aesthetic Perception* (Champaign: University of Illinois Press, 1969).

18. Blink Twice website (http://www.blink-twice.com).

19. Jesse Ashlock, "The Great Communicator," *I.D. Magazine* (May 2006).

20. Alan Pipes, *Production for Graphic Designers* (London: Laurence King, 2005) p. 168.

21. Craftspace website (http://www.craftspace.co.uk)

22. Deirdre Buckley, Jac Fennell, and Deirdre Figueiredo, "Designing for Access: Young Disabled People as Active Participants Influencing Design Processes" (paper presented at Include, Royal College of Art, London, April 5–8, 2005).

Tomoko Azumi meets step stools

1. Sandy Marshall, "I Am 4ft 2in," *Guardian*, September 17, 2005.

2. Michael Shamash, personal communication, November 10, 2006

3. Alex Wiltshire, "Shin and Tomoko Azumi," *Icon Magazine* 013 (June 2004).

4. Tomoko Azumi's website (http://www.tnadesignstudio.co.uk).

5. David Sokol, "Lone Star," *I.D. Magazine* (June 2006).

6. Ibid., 3.

if Philippe Starck met bottom wipers

1. BIME website (http://www.bath.ac.uk/bime/products/dl_products. htm).

2. Successive speakers made dismissive references to Starck at Include 2007, the International Conference on Inclusive Design, Royal College of Art, London, April 2–4, 2007.

Michael Marriott meets wheelchairs

1. Michael Marriott interviewed for the Design Museum. London and the British Council on the Design Museum website (http://www. designmuseum.org/design/michael-marriott).

2. Michael Marriott, personal communication, June 12, 2006.

3. Marcel Duchamp, quoted on MoMA website (http://www.moma. org/collection/browse_results.php?object_id=81631).

4. Clare Catterall, *Specials: New Graphics* (London: Booth-Clibborn Editions, 2001).

if Hussein Chalayan met robot arms

1. Michael Hillman, "Rehabilitation Robotics from Past to Present: A Historical Perspective," in *Proceedings of the ICORR 2003 (eighth International Conference on Rehabilitation Robotics)*, Daejeon, Korea, April 23–25, 2003 (Daejeon, Korea: HWRS-ERC). See also BIME website (http://www. bath.ac.uk/bime/projects/as_projects.htm).

2. Susannah Frankel, "Fashion: Perfect Ten," *Independent* (April 23, 2005).

3. Regine Debatty on We Make Money Not Art website (http://www. we-make-money-not-art.com/archives/2005/10/his-autumnwinte.php).

Martin Bone meets prosthetic legs

1. Martin Bone, personal communication, August 20, 2007.

2. Ibid.

3. Ibid.

4. Ibid.

5. Ibid.

6. Ibid.

7. Ibid.

if Cutler and Gross met hearing aids

1. Tony Gross, personal communication, April 4, 2007.

Graphic Thought Facility meets braille

1. Huw Morgan and Andy Stevens, personal communication, October 6, 2006.

2. Ibid.

3. Ibid.

4. Ibid.

Crispin Jones meets watches for visually impaired people

1. Fondation de la haute horlogerie website (http://www.hautehorlogerie.org/en/encyclopaedia/glossary/tact-watch.html).

2. Quoted in Crispin Jones, Mr Jones Watches, (London: Crispin Jones, 2004). See also Crispin Jones's website (http://www.mr-jones.org/watches/index.htm).

3. Crispin Jones, personal communication, August 31, 2007.

4. Ibid.

Andrew Cook meets communication aids

1. Andrew Cook, personal communication, September 5, 2007.

2. Ibid.

3. Ibid.

if Stefan Sagmeister met accessibility signage

1. Peter Hall and Stefan Sagmeister, Made You Look (London: Booth–Clibborn Editions, 2001).

2. Ibid., p. 171.

Vexed meets wheelchair capes

1. Joe Hunter and Adam Thorpe, personal communication, October 5, 2007.

2. Ibid.

3. Ibid.

4. Ibid.

5. Ibid.

6. Ibid.

7. Ibid.

8. Ibid.

9. Ibid.

10. Ibid.

conclusion

1. Jonathan Ive interviewed for the Design Museum as part of "25/25: Celebrating 25 Years of Design," Design Museum, London, March 29–June 22, 2007, on Design Museum website (http://www. designmuseum.org/design/jonathan-ive).

2. Ibid.

3. Madame L'Amic of the Musée des Arts Décoratifs in Paris, interviewing Charles Eames for the exhibition catalog for "What Is Design?" (1968), reprinted in John Neuhart, Marilyn Neuhart, and Ray Eames, *Eames Design: The Work of the Office of Charles and Ray Eames* (New York: Harry N. Abrams Inc., 1989).

photography credits

Photo: author, courtesy of Eames Office LLC x

Photo: Hans Hansen © Vitra, courtesy of Herman Miller and Vitra xii

Photo: courtesy of Eames Office xiv

Photo: Platon, courtesy of Cutler and Gross 14

Photo: Platon, courtesy of Cutler and Gross 18

Photo: Tim Kavanagh/RNID 20

Photo: Tim Kavanagh/RNID 22

Photo: Jonny Thompson/RNID 24

Photo: Tim Kavanagh/RNID 26

Photo: Nick Knight/NK Image, courtesy of Aimee Mullins 30

Photo: Aimee Mullins 32

Photo: Jean-Claude Revy/ SPL 34

Photo: Jean-Claude Revy/ SPL 36

Photo: Yoneo Kawabe © nextmaruni 40

Photo: V&A Images/Victoria and Albert Museum 42

Photo: Wellcome Library, London 44

Photo: Michael Cullen, courtesy of Knoll, Inc. 46

Photo: courtesy of RGK Wheelchairs Ltd. 48

Photo: Tom Metcalfe 50

Photo: Yoneo Kawabe © nextmaruni 52

Photo: Yoneo Kawabe © nextmaruni 54

Photo: David Constantine/Motivation 56

Photo: Lon van Keulen, featured in *Interior View* 14, "Blind Design,"
courtesy of <http://www.edelkoort.com> 58

Photo: Lon van Keulen, courtesy of <http://www.edelkoort.com> 60

Photo: Graeme Duddridge 62

Photo: Mikkel Koser 66

Photo: Mikkel Koser 68

Photo: Mikkel Koser 72

Photo: courtesy of Leckey and Triplicate 74

Photo: Mikkel Koser 78

Photo: courtesy of BIME 82

Photo: Sasaki Hidetoyo, courtesy of IDEO 84

Photo: author, courtesy of IDEO 88

Photo: courtesy of Tissot 96

Illustration: © Crispin Jones, courtesy of the artist   98

Illustration: © Crispin Jones, courtesy of the artist   100

Photo: Jonny Thompson/RNID   104

Photo: Lucy Andrews, courtesy of IDEO   106

Photo: Marc Quinn Studio © the artist, courtesy of
Jay Jopling/White Cube (London)   112

Photo: courtesy of the artist, restored by Sarah McMichael; in the
collection of the Crafts Council, London   114

Photo: courtesy of the artist and Catherine Long; commissioned
by the City Gallery, Leicester, for "Adorn, Equip"   116

Photo: Rob Hann, courtesy of the artist and Mat Fraser;
commissioned by the City Gallery, Leicester, for "Adorn, Equip"   118

Photo: Jason Evans, courtesy of Dunne & Raby   120

Photo: Toshihiro Komatsu, courtesy of Kelly Dobson   124

Photo: Maura Shea, courtesy of IDEO and Crispin Jones   128

Photo: Maura Shea, courtesy of IDEO and Crispin Jones   130

Photo: Crispin Jones, courtesy of IDEO   136

Photo: Jason Tozer, courtesy of IDEO   140

Photo: Interaction Research Studio, Goldsmiths, University of
London, courtesy of Bill Gaver; used with permission   148

Photo: Interaction Research Studio, Goldsmiths, University of
London, courtesy of Bill Gaver; used with permission   150

Photo: Jason Evans, courtesy of Dunne & Raby   152

Photo: author, courtesy of IDEO   156

Photo: author, courtesy of Cambridge University Press   160

Photo: Maura Shea, courtesy of IDEO   162

Photo: Maura Shea, courtesy of IDEO   164

Photo: Evan Kafka, courtesy of the artists   168

Illustration: Urtica   170

Photo: courtesy of Blink Twice   172

Photo: Johanna Van Daalen, courtesy of electricwig, Craftspace,
and Somiya Shabban   174

Photo: Johanna Van Daalen, courtesy of electricwig and Craftspace   176

Illustration: Vexed Design   182

Photo: Yoneo Kawabe © nextmaruni   184

Photo: Andrew Buurman	186
Photo: courtesy of the designer	188
Photo: Yoneo Kawabe © nextmaruni	190
Photo: Barbara Etter, courtesy of t.n.a. Design Studio	194
Illustration: © Tomoko Azumi, courtesy of the designer	196–197
Photo: courtesy of S+ARCKNetwork	198
Photo: Studio One, courtesy of the designer	200
Photo: courtesy of the designer	202
Photo: courtesy of RGK Wheelchairs Ltd.	204
Photo: Michael Marriott	206
Photo: Michael Marriott	208
Illustration: © Michael Marriott, courtesy of the designer	210
Illustration: Michael Marriott, courtesy of the designer	214–215
Photo: AP Photo/Alastair Grant, courtesy of PA Photos	216
Photo: Rick English, courtesy of IDEO	218
Photo: © Otto Bock, courtesy of Otto Bock HealthCare GmbH	220
Photo: courtesy of IDEO	222
Photo: Martin Bone, courtesy of the designer	224
Photo: © Martin Bone, courtesy of the designer	230–231
Photo: courtesy of Apple Inc.	232
Photo: courtesy of Paul Smith Ltd.	234
Photo: Kirby Koh, courtesy of Cutler and Gross	236
Photo: courtesy of GTF	238
Photo: courtesy of GTF	240
Photo: courtesy of GTF	242
Photo: courtesy of GTF	244
Photo: Lubna Chowdhary, courtesy of the artist	246
Illustration: © GTF, courtesy of GTF	250–251
Photo: courtesy of Studio Tord Boontje	252
Photo: Crispin Jones, courtesy of the designer	254
Photo: V&A Images/Victoria and Albert Museum	256
Photo: Andrew Powell, courtesy of the designer	258
Photo: courtesy of Crispin Jones	260
Illustration: © Crispin Jones, courtesy of the designer	264–265
Photo: Thomas Stewart, courtesy of IDEO	266

Photo: courtesy of the artist   268

Photo: Paul Gault, courtesy of the designer   270

Photo: courtesy of Toby Churchill Ltd.   272

Photo: Paul Gault, courtesy of Mast   274

Photo: Andrew Cook   276

Photo: Eugene Lee, courtesy of the artist   278

Illustration: © Andrew Cook, courtesy of the designer   282–283

Photo: Jason Evans, courtesy of Dunne & Raby   284

Photo: Tom Schierlitz, courtesy of the designer   286

Photo: courtesy of Vexed Design   288

Photo: courtesy of Vexed Design   290

Photo: courtesy of Vexed Design   292

Photo: courtesy of Vexed Design   294

Illustration: © Vexed Design, courtesy of Vexed Design   298–299

Photo: Ssam sungun Kim, courtesy of Cutler and Gross.

Make-up: Kavita Kaul.   302

Photo: courtesy of Apple Inc.   304

Photo: Hans Hansen © Vitra, courtesy of Herman Miller and Vitra   306

index

AAC, 157–179, 267, 269, 271–283

Ability, 89. *See also* Disability

Able-bodied, 33, 89, 91, 93. *See also* Nondisabled

Abstraction, 227

Accessibility, 80, 85. *See also* Disability

signage, 287

Achondroplasia, 187

Acoustic throne, 107

Adjustability, 76

Adoption, of prototypes, 151–153

Adorn, Equip, 119, 121

Aesthetics, 178–179. *See also* Design

Aha, 171

Alison Lapper Pregnant, 112, 117

All things to all people, 69, 85

Alm, Norman, 165

Ambiguity, 122, 173

Anderson, Laurie, 167

Antidesign, 212

Apple, 68–72, 77–79, 232–233, 303–305

Appliances, 71, 73

Archetypal chairs, 53

Artificiality, 35, 167

Artificial limb. *See also* Prostheses workshop, 117

Artistic appreciation, 83

Artists, 115, 117, 268–269

Assistive products, 92

Assistive technology, 2, 217, 261, 297

Attention to detail, 19, 209

Attention to hidden details, 235

Audiobooks, 95

Audiophilia, 95

Augmentative and Alternative Communication. *See* AAC

Azumi, Shin, 52–53

Azumi, Tomoko, 52–53, 184–197

Background noise, 105

Badge, 174, 176–177

Bath chairs, 47

Bath Institute of Medical Engineering. *See* BIME

Bespoke legs, 225

Bicycle Wheel, 211

Bicycle wheels, 55, 205–215

BIME, 81, 146–147, 187

Bishop, Durrell, 266–267

Blankinship, Erik, 165–166

Blind Design, 61

BlindKiss, 80, 131–132, 261

BlindStation, 95

Blink Twice, 173, 175

Bone, Martin, 218–231

Boontje, Tord, 243–245, 252–253

Bosher, Peter, 73

Bottom wiper, 199

Braille, 253

blowing up, 248–251

Braille-Lite, 73

dress, 58, 61

mechanical, 257

for the sighted, 59–63

signage, 240–251

wall, 248–251

Braille-like, 63, 243

Bray, Duane, 144–145

Breuer, Marcel, 47

Buchanan, Jamie, 105

Buchenau, Marion, 141

Camouflage, 15, 18, 28

Carbon fiber legs, 30–31

CD player, 83

Cell phones, 127–131

Ceramic

    braille, 248–251

    hearing aid, 307

    tiles, 247

Cerebral palsy, 75–76, 165

Chairs

    1,000 chairs, 51

    acoustic throne, 107

    archetypal Japanese, 53

    Bath chair, 47

    DCW, xiii

    evolution, 51

    Forgotten Chairs, 51

    Gentleman's chair, 50

    Herman Miller, xiii

    nextmaruni, 53

    Wassily, 47

    wheelchairs (*see* Wheelchairs)

    Woosh, 74

    XL1 Kit, 206–207

Chalayan, Hussein, 216–217

Chowdhary, Lubna, 246, 247

Churchill, Toby, 267, 272

Clinical trials, 137

Coffee tables

    ballooning, 149

    telescoping, 217

Cognitive impairment, 85, 285

Colours randomly chosen, 132

Communication. *See also* AAC

    engaging, 158

    unambiguous, 158

Communication aids, 157–179,

    267, 269, 271–283

Complex communication needs,

    158. *See also* AAC

Concealment, 23

Constantine, David, 55–57, 201

Contextual disability, 91

Cook, Andrew, 270–283

Craftspace, 177

Critical design, 121–133, 151,

    259–261, 285

Crystal, David, 159

Cultural diversity, 89

Cultural divisions, 103

Cultural references, 21

Cultural tension, 15

Curious Home, The, 149–151

Cutler, Graham, 21

Cutler and Gross, 14, 18, 21,

    236–237, 302

Dark chocolate, 280

Dark humor, 127

Dazed & Confused, 29–30

Deafness, 102

Deaf with a capital D, 102–103,

    237

Deaf with a little d, 102, 105, 237

Decoration, 253

Dementia, 81–83, 146–147

Design

for all, 101

that asks questions, 121

awards, 69, 75–76

constraints, xiii

critical, 121–133, 151,
259–261, 285

for disability, 2

engineering, 49, 212, 303

ethnography, 90

exploration, xv, 43–64

fashion, 13–38, 216–217,
234–235, 237, 288–299,
303

furniture, xi–xv, 51–55, 57,
59, 184–197, 200–215

good, xi

graphic, 175, 238–251,
286–287

inclusive, 2, 67

industrial, 24–28, 70, 83–85,
173–175, 218–233,
252–253, 266–267

interaction, 70, 94–101,
127–131, 138–139,
144–145, 149–151,
161–164, 169–171,
254–267, 270–283

interdisciplinary, 214, 303

interior, 241

language, 233

ludic, 151

mainstream, 2

resonant, 93, 109, 297

for special needs, 2

standards, 51

universal, 2, 67

user-centered, 90

What Is Design?, 305

for the whole population, 67

Designing for Access, 177

Dictionary of Primal Behaviour,
171–173

Disability

achondroplasia, 187

amputees, 28–37, 219–231

arm movement, 217

cerebral palsy, 75–76, 165

cognitive impairment, 85, 285

complex communication
needs, 157–179, 267, 269,
271–283

contextual, 91

definition, 1, 91

dementia, 81–83, 146–147

hearing impairment, 23–28,
101–105, 126, 233, 235,
237

medical model, 19, 47, 205

mobility impairment, 42,
44–49, 55–57

phocomelia, 117

restricted growth, 187

restricted reach, 199

signage, 287

speech impairment, 267, 269,
271–283

upper limb disablement, 217

visual impairment, 16–23,
    61, 73, 80, 93–101,
    131–132, 240–251,
    255–265
Disabled people, 2. *See also* Disability
Discretion, 15
Diversity, 89, 183
Dobson, Kelly, 123–124
Dover Street Market, 237
Drift Table, 149–151
Duchamp, Marcel, 210–215
Dunne, Anthony, 121–122
Dunne & Raby, 121–122, 151,
    284–285

Eames, Charles, xiii, 305
Eames, Charles and Ray, xi–xv,
    306–307
Eames, Ray, xv
Edelkoort, Li, 61
Eerily realistic, 167
Electric Shock Mobile, The, 127–129
Electricwig, 177
Electro-draft Excluder, 151
Ellenson, Richard, 173–175
Emotional response, 83
Enfants terribles, 21, 59, 305
Engineering brilliance, 303
Ephemeral kiss, 169
Ephemeral speech, 269
Everest & Jennings, 47
Experience prototyping, 139–145
Expressive gestures, 171
Eyes-free interaction, 94
Eyewear, 18–23. *See also* Glasses

Facial expressions, 163
Fake, 221
Fashion, 13–38
Fashion-able?, 29
Fashion designers, 29–33, 216–217,
    234–235, 288–299, 303
Fashion retail, 236–237
Figueiredo, Dierdre, 177
First impressions, 175
Fitness for purpose, 67
Flagiello, Caroline, 105
Flesh-colored plastic, 235
Flying submarine, 75–76
Forgotten materials, 223
Fox, Shelley, 61
Fraser, Mat, 119
Frayling, Christopher, 75
Frivolity, 125
Fukasawa, Naoto, 83
Fulton-Suri, Jane, 141
Furniture
    acoustic throne, 107
    chairs (*see* Chairs)
    for children with cerebral
      palsy, 75–76
    coffee tables, 149, 217
    Drift Table, 149–151
    interactive, 149–151
    Milan fair, 51
    step stools, 185–197
    Table = Chest, 188–189
    Table Talk, 105–108
    wheelchairs (*see* Wheelchairs)
Furniture designers, xi–xv, 51–55,
    57, 59, 184–197, 200–215

Garden shed, 226

Garland lamp shade, 252–253

Gaver, Bill, 148–151

Gizmo, 73

Glasses

    camouflage, 18

    Cutler and Gross, 14, 18, 21, 236–237

    Eastman, 218, 223

    eyewear, 18–23

    materiality, 17

    National Health Service spectacles, 16–18

    nonprescription lenses, 17

    pink plastic, 17

    sunglasses, 218, 223

    surround sound, 20

Glass legs, 33

Gloucester smart house, 146–147

Gold earpieces, 27

Golden hand, 34–37

Goldsmiths College, 149–151

Gosling, Ju, 121

Graphic designers, 175, 238–251, 286–287

Graphic Thought Facility, 238–251

Gregorian chant, 167

Gross, Tony, 21, 237

H2.0 symposium, 33

Hand-carved wooden legs, 31

Hand controllers, 143

Hand-ear coordination, 95

Hand of Good, Hand of God, 119

Hands

    abstraction, 119

    bespoke, 226

    clammy, 35

    expression, 171

    golden, 35–37

    pink plastic, 35, 37

    rubbery, 35

    split hooks, 35

Hansen, Mark, 167–168

Hard of hearing, 102. *See also* Disability, hearing impairment

Hawking, Stephen, 166

Health Buddy, 144–145

Hearing, 103

Hearing aids, 23–28, 126, 233, 235, 237, 305, 307

    concealment, 23

    Deaf with a capital D, 102

    evolution, 23

    HearWear, 25–28

    miniaturization, 23

    pink plastic, 23, 28

Hearing impairment, 23–28, 101–105, 126, 233, 235, 237

Hearing technology, 25–27, 107

HearWear, 25–28, 126

Hecht, Sam, 27

Herman Miller, xiii

Herr, Hugh, 33–35, 221

Hidden detail, 235

Hocking, Clare, 125

Holmes, John, 159

Honeyman, Art, 165–166
Hulger, 28
Hunter, Joe, 293–299
Hunter, Mat, 138

Iconoclasm, 287, 303
IDEO, 93, 101–108, 127–131,
      138–145, 221–223
Impairment, definition, 1. *See also*
      Disability
Inclusive design, 2, 67
Induction loop, 107
Industrial designers, 24–28, 70,
      83–85, 173–175, 198–199,
      218–233, 252–253,
      266–267
Industrial Facility, 20, 27
Insensitivity, 125
Interaction designers, 70, 99–101,
      127–131, 138–139,
      144–145, 149–151,
      161–164, 169–171,
      254–267, 270–283
Interaction Research Studio,
      149–151
International Classification of
      Functioning, Disability and
      Health (ICF), 91
Intonation, 165, 277. *See also* Voice,
      tone of
   diagrams, 159–160
Invisible hearing aids, 15
Invisible radiation, 151
iPhone, 71–73
iPod, 69–71, 77–79, 232–233

Iterative user testing, 146
Ive, Jonathan, 70–71, 232–233,
      303–305, 307

Jobs, Steve, 79
Johnson, Paul, 165
Jones, Crispin, 98–101, 127–131,
      136, 254–265

Kerr, Duncan, 138–139, 169–171
Kiss Communicator, 169–171
Knitwear, 61, 119

Lapper, Alison, 117
Latif, Amar, 163
Leckey, James, 75–76
Legs
   bespoke, 225
   carbon fiber, 30–31
   cosmetic, 31, 221
   glass, 33
   hand-carved wooden, 31–32
   men's, 225
   Otto Bock, 220
   polka dot, 33
   prosthetic, 29–35, 217–231
   silicone, 31
   women's, 225
   wooden, 31–32, 225
Leg splint, xi
Lightness of touch, 85
Lightwriter, 267
Limbs. *See also* Prostheses
   cosmetic, 31
   functional, 31

prosthetic, 28–37

Lip-reading, 105

Listening Post, 167

Long, Catherine, 119

Lovegrove, Ross, 22, 24, 27

Ludic design, 151

Macabre, 167

Mainstream design, defined, 2

Marriott, Michael, 202–215

Marshall, Sandy, 186–187

Martin, Heather, 169–171

Materiality, 17, 221

McQueen, Alexander, 29

Medical model, 19, 47, 205

Meetings with designers, 181–299

Memory aids, 146–147, 285

Milan furniture fair, 51

Miniaturization, 23

MIT Media Lab, 33, 123,
    165–166, 221

Modularity, 76

Monestier, Jacques, 35–37

Moon writing, 61

Morgan, Huw, 245, 247–251

Morrison, Jasper, 53–54, 200–201

Motivation, 55, 201

Moulton, Alex, 211–215

Mr Jones Watches, 254, 258–259

Muji CD player, 83

Mullins, Aimee, 29–33, 221

Newell, Alan, 92, 161

Nextmaruni, 53

Ninja fleece, 293

Noisy environment, 105

Nondisabled, 92. *See also* Ablebodied

Older people, 145

Open Source Prosthetics, 226

Optometry, 21

Orpwood, Roger, 83, 146–147,
    187

Otto Bock, 220

Paralinguistic, 163

Patients, 16

People
    with dementia, 81–83,
        146–147
    with disabilities, 2 (*see also*
        Disability)
    disabled, 2 (*see also* Disability)
    older, 145
    with restricted growth, 187
    with restricted reach, 199
    visually impaired, 93–101,
        240–251 (*see also* Disability,
        visual impairment)

People first language, 2

Performance, 277

Petrie, Helen, 147

Phocomelia, 117

Pigeonhole, 3

Pink plastic, 15
    glasses, 17
    hands, 35, 37
    hearing aids, 23

Placebo, 151

Platforms, 71

Playful exploration, xv, 41, 149

PlayStation, 142, 175. *See also*
    BlindStation

Pleasure, 305

Plywood
    forming, xi–xv
    furniture, xiii
    leg splint, xi
    sculpture, xv

Poetry, 165–166
    in mundane products, 199

Popp, Julius, 268–269

Prepared piano, 279

Pretty, 43, 63

Problem solving, 41

Prostheses
    artificial limb workshop, 117
    climbing, 33
    cosmetic, 31
    emotional, 123
    functional, 31, 221
    hands, 35–37
    legs, 29–35, 219–231
    limbs, 28–37
    Open Source, 226
    split hooks, 35
    running, 31

Prosthetic. *See* Prostheses

Prototypes, 137–153
    adoption, 153
    behaves-like, 141
    early, 139
    experience, 139–145
    looks-like, 141
    preproduction, 139

quick-and-dirty, 145
    Wizard of Oz, 144

Punctuation, 159

Quinn, Marc, 117

Rabin, Antony, 102

Raby, Fiona, 121

Radio dials, 95

Radio prompts, 147

Radios
    Digital Audio Broadcasting, 79
    iconic, 81
    simple, 81
    single-station, 81
    Teddy Blood Bag, 284

Really, seventeen ways to say, 165

Resonant design, 92–94, 109, 297

Restricted growth, 187, 189

Restricted reach, 199

RNIB, 97–99, 131–132, 247, 257

RNID, 25, 101–102, 104–105

RNLI, 131

Robins, Freddie, 119

Roope, Nic, 28

Rose, Damon, 131

Royal College of Art, 75, 121, 189,
    207, 226, 245

Rubbery hands, 35

Rubin, Ben, 167–168

Sablé, Sebastien, 95

Safecracking, 95

Sagmeister, Stefan, 286–287

Sarcasm, 159

Scream Body, 123

Sculpture, xiv–xv, 115

Self-expression, 171

Self-image, 259

Sensitivity, 113

Shabban, Somiya, 177

Shamash, Michael, 189

Short Armed and Dangerous, 119

Simple radios, 81

Simplicity, 67–86

Sitting to attention, 57, 201

Smart homes, 125

Smith, Paul, 234–235

Social Mobiles, 127–131, 161–164

Social model, 19, 47

Sod off, 177

Solving problems, 41

Speaking Mobile, The, 161–164

Spectacles. See Glasses

Speech technology, 80

Sperlein, Bodo, 63

Spiekermann, Erik, 175

Spimes, 75

Split hooks, 35

Spyfish STV, 141–143

Starck, Philippe, 198–199

Step stools, 185–197

Stereotype, 49, 89, 177

Sterling, Bruce, 73

Stevens, Andy, 243–251

Subjectivity, 144

Submarine

    flying, 75–76

    PlayStation game, 142

    telepresence vehicle, 141–143

Superhuman hearing, 103

Supersafe products, 132

Swiss Army knife, 71

Table = Chest, 188–189

Table Talk, 105–108

Tactile map, 247

Tactile watches, 97–101

Tactophonics, 270, 273–277

Talking user interface, 80

Talking watches, 97, 257

Tango!, 172–173, 175

Tensions

    cultural, 15

    healthy, xv

    initial, 4, 11–179

Terrible affliction, 131

Text-to-speech, 159

Therapeutic excellence, 303

Thompson, Henrietta, 25

Thorpe, Adam, 293–299

Tissot, 97–99

Titanium steel, 209

Toby Churchill, 267

Tone of voice, 159, 193, 267, 277

Trendy nose pegs, 132

Trickle-down effect, xiii

Trimpin, 278, 280

Trite logos, 287

Tubular steel, 47

Tyler, Steve, 73, 99

Typography, 267

Uh-huh, 163

Universal design, 2, 67

University of Dundee, 51, 81, 92, 161, 165, 273

Urban culture, 297

Urban mobility cape, 296

Urtica, 171–173

Usability lab, 144

User-centered design, 90

User interfaces. *See also* Design, interaction

  accessibility, 80

  auditory, 80

  nonvisual, 94

  radio, 80

  screen-based, 95

  talking, 80

User testing, 144, 146

Utopian vision, 121

Van Daalen, Johanna, 177

Venus de Milo, 117

Veterans Association, 47

Vexed, 288–299

Victoria & Albert Museum, 151

Visually impaired design team, 94

Visually impaired people, 16–23, 61, 73, 80, 94–101, 131–132, 241, 247, 253, 255–265

Voice

  dark chocolate, 280

  disembodied, 146–147

  find their voice, 178

  his, 166

  monotonic, 167

  rich fruitcake, 280

synthetic, 167

  tone of, 159

Voice-enabled PDA, 93

Voice output communication aids, 157

Vojvodic, Violeta, 171–173

Waller, Annalu, 165

Wassily chair, 47

Wastefulness, 125

Watches, 97–99, 101, 254–265

  audible, 257

  Discretion Watch, The, 101

  Humility Watch, The, 259

  Personality Watch, The, 259

  RNIB, 97–99, 257

  Silen-T, 97–99

  à tact, 101

  tactile, 97, 257

  talking, 97

  Tissot, 97–99

Waterproof, 291

Wearer, 19, 57, 259

Wheelchair access, 287

Wheelchair capes, 289–299

Wheelchairs, 45–49, 55–59, 201, 203–215

  basketball, 47

  Bath chairs, 47

  bicycle wheels, 55

  Cambodia, 55

  convergence, 45–49

  Everest & Jennings, 47

  in low-income countries, 55

  Motivation, 55–57

posture, 57

RGK Interceptor, 48, 204

sports, 47

three-wheeled, 55

titanium steel, 209

tropical hardwood, 55

tubular steel, 47

welded metal, 55

WHO, 1, 91

Without thought, 83

Wizard of Oz prototypes, 144

Wood

Bath chairs, 47

clogs, 278, 280

furniture, xiii

hand-carved legs, 31

hardwood composite, 223

legs, 31, 225

leg splint, xi

nextmaruni chairs, 53

plywood forming, xi–xv

sandalwood watch, 261

sculpture, xv

tiered skirt, 216–217

wheelchair for Cambodia, 55

World Health Organization. *See*
WHO

Writing

Moon, 61

space, 247

Yes

nine ways to say, 159

sort of . . ., 163

ye-yeah, 163

You cannot not communicate, 175

Yuck, 171–173

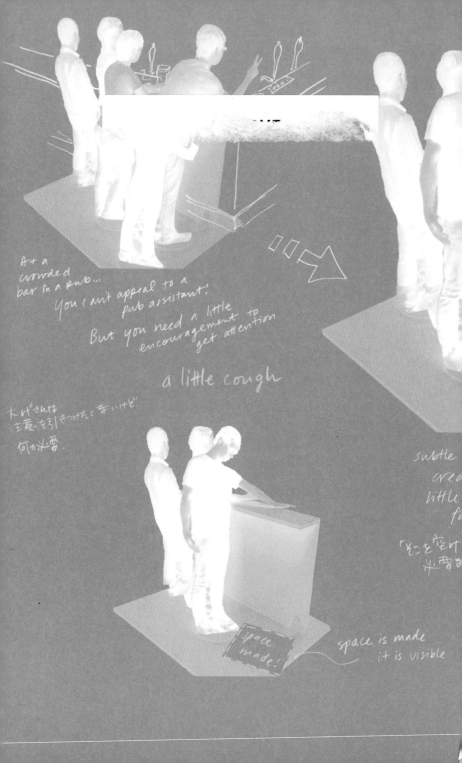

At a
crowded
bar in a pub...
You can't appeal to a
    pub assistant!
But you need a little
   encouragement to
      get attention

a little cough

大げさには
注意を引きつけたくないけど!
何か火雲.

subtle
   crea
   little
      fo
「そこを空け
   火雲ま

space is made!

space is made
   it is visible